Meh, Good Enough

A Veteran's Lessons from the Private Sector

Noah Johnson

www.VLUGRD.com

Phoenix, Arizona

Meh, Good Enough is a work of nonfiction but certain names of nonpublic figures have been changed, and some of the private individuals described are fictionalized or composite portraits.

Copyright © 2023 by Noah Johnson All rights reserved.

Published in the United States by VLUGRD, LLC.

ISBN 979-8-9894797-1-9

Cover Design by Noah Johnson

www.VLUGRD.com

Business, Career, Leadership, Military Transition, Finance, Investing, Planning, Budgeting, Values, Veteran, Real Estate, Data, Banking, Lending, Economy, Risk, Power Belly, Statistics, Nepotism, Attribution, Biases, Research.

To Sadie

Content

Chapter 1: Good Enough 9

Chapter 2: Source Data.......................... 17

Chapter 3: Value................................... 32

Chapter 4: Everything is a Tradeoff 57

Chapter 5: Do Something, but Don't Do *Anything* 69

Chapter 6: Statistics Matter 92

Chapter 7: To Be or Seem to Be, that is the Question 100

Chapter 8: Fit-ness Matters 111

Chapter 9: Opportunity.................................... 123

Chapter 10: Personality-Driven Success............ 134

Chapter 11: The Working Class Works too Hard 143

Chapter 12: The Working Class Must Work Harder 157

Chapter 13: Being Good May Mean Sucking at Your Job 163

Chapter 14: Don't Care More than Your Manager 178

Chapter 15: Nepotism 182

Chapter 16: Attribution Bias 195

Chapter 17: Join the Military 208

Chapter 18: Leadership 218

Chapter 19: Dig Deeper 239

Preface

The private sector does not reward hard work unless you consider more work for the same pay a reward. You didn't think I would claim it's a meritocracy, did you? Individual effort matters, but there is so much more to get right.

What else is there? That's what we'll explore.

This book is a must-read before you apply for a job, negotiate a salary, attempt a promotion, invest, buy a house, choose a college degree, get married, select your industry or field, and most importantly, before separating from the military. If you want an author to tout your military experience and how it easily relates to jobs in the private sector, go buy a different book. The private sector does not care about your service, no matter how much they profess their love for it. Plus, how does making you feel good help you improve? If you're so great already, you don't need my assistance.

I struggled after separating from the U.S. Air Force – how do I get a good job, earn a promotion, or stay employed during a recession, were questions I didn't have answers to. Hard work is simply not enough. The military has its challenges but provides everything one needs: food, shelter, training, purpose, and a guide to creating a fruitful career. You are alone to figure out life in the private sector. Well, almost alone. Many books claim to help you figure it all out but have little tangible value beyond making you feel good; many of them written by people who have never lived in the real world. This is why I chose a different strategy.

A framework is required to make good decisions consistently. Good decisions help us obtain what we desire, whatever it is. Here, I provide such a framework to help veterans, current service members, and civilians navigate the private sector. This is not a book about success. I have never achieved great success. I am not *wealthy*. I'm a relatively normal guy. I grew up working class, enlisted in the U.S. Air Force, separated, struggled, invested, failed, wanted more, and worked my way up from the working class and near homelessness through the middle class and into the upper middle class. I was challenged to find what I wanted and had no framework for viewing the world without the military guiding me. I am not the only person in this position, as many millennials have struggled with the same issues. Veterans of all ages are most vulnerable to these challenges due to the different military and private sector incentives, but there are lessons for everyone here.

I've experienced the various socioeconomic classes firsthand, from being unemployed with a network of similarly unemployed/underemployed, to being in the upper middle class with a network of well-employed bankers and medical doctors. This has taught me many lessons; the utmost is that wanting more and not achieving it is heartbreaking and demoralizing. These feelings imperil everything we do, festering deep confusion over what we're doing wrong. I am not alone in learning this, but many others have yet to find their way. Obviously, the other key lesson is that finding what we want is very possible with the right actions. This is why I share my framework with you – to help you on the path to *the good life* in the private sector.

I do not rely on get-rich-quick schemes. If something sounds too good to be true, it is. Or, it requires luck. I am not lucky. I hope you are, but you are probably not, either. You don't need luck to be happy if you know what matters. This is why I focus on replicable actions that provide a consistent outcome – no luck is required.

My framework involves the following assumptions:
> 1. You need to know what you want.
> 2. You should work to obtain what you want (align your actions to your values, goals, and desires).
> 3. There are constraints to getting what you want.
> 4. You have levers to pull that remove or mitigate most constraints.
> 5. Time and effort are always required.

I will delve into each of these.

This book only intends to provoke thought to guide your judgment, not to prescribe specific advice. It is designed to help you determine your values and goals that will assist you in becoming who you are meant to be by making solid decisions. You have or will encounter many of the same situations, and I hope my perspective assists your self- reflection. I illustrate events from my life to help you conceptualize the point I am trying to make – not to deprecate or brag, but to provide an honest perspective. This is not about how special I am; the only notable thing I ever did was learn from my mistakes and continue trying. I also took pretty good notes and had a strong network of people to learn from. Wisdom is found all over if you keep an open mind, so I also use examples from current events and pop culture.

It took me a long time to find *the good life*. I got divorced after leaving the military, switched college majors many times, had no idea what I wanted or how to obtain what I wanted, graduated with a useless Bachelor of Arts degree, thought I was special and entitled to more, switched jobs several times, started a few companies, failed, married again, returned to college for a useful degree, divorced again, found my dream career, found my dream woman, still struggled a bit, bought a beautiful house, got married again, learned more tangible skills remodeling, *built* a fantastic home, had my first child, learned what matters, stopped struggling, and found what I wanted. My life turned around due to living the concepts in this book, and I hope to help you do the same. Surviving is not enough – *thriving* is the goal.

This is not a linear story. Chapters are composed of key concepts to which I relate experiences and events. I round it all off at the end to bring the framework full circle.

I will tell you about what something *is*, but I will also tell you a lot about what something *is not*. It is often easier to learn from the negative than the positive, just like you may learn more from a lousy manager than a good one. Learning what not to do may be more beneficial and universally applicable than knowing what to do. For example, it is easy to understand why you should not smoke crack. But what to do instead has nearly infinite possibilities; where would I begin? This is why a framework is essential; it does not tell you what to do but guides you in analyzing and choosing your best options, no matter the circumstance. (Don't worry; my lessons are more sophisticated than advice on recreational drug use.)

If you haven't noticed already, I say *you* a lot. *You* are the general audience, not necessarily the individual reading this book. *You* are the statistically average reader.

I use a conversational style of writing some people find irritating for its lack of formality and loose grammar (or, as my wife says, "poor" grammar). I write how I speak. I ask questions

Preface

and use colloquial language. You will also notice I use definitive language. If I say something *is*, I mean it generally *is*. Is it true in every scenario? Probably not. I am sure you will know that one person who contradicts some of my general statements. Again, what I seek is replicability. If that person's achievement is replicable, great. Use them as an example for your life. Replicability is a key theme of this book.

Provided here are many examples of familiar narratives perpetuated by the media, leaders, politicians, and businesses regarding success. These narratives are spread to give people hope but have no real substance. Most are harmful to ordinary people and serve to feed on our naivete, ignorance, and greed, all of which are expected when regular people are force-fed stories of so many others getting more for less effort. We feel like we're being left out or FOMO. This is all contrived by the originators of the narratives to get you to act for their benefit. I detest most success narratives and work to illustrate that the narratives and the perpetuators are full of shit – this realization is necessary for long-term sustainable performance. I'm not a curmudgeon, just a pragmatist. This is a pragmatic guide for life in the private sector.

Actually, my wife just reminded me that I am a curmudgeon, and this is the cynic's guide to the private sector.

You want to be an Electrical Engineer but aren't willing to go to college? Sorry, but you're not going to get there. You want to be a world-famous athlete? Sorry, you're not going to get there either. (Yes, I recognize there are many famous athletes, but that doesn't mean *you* have a shot.) You may as well strive to be a lottery winner and spend your energy and money buying tickets. I don't work on luck; I work on method and replicability. You could do everything Lebron

James did to become a world-class athlete and never achieve anywhere near the success he has. That doesn't mean you should not dream big, but I'll elaborate on why thinking you're special and focusing your energy on becoming rich and famous is a bad bet.

It would help if you made notes about your thoughts as you read through this, but not about any specific fact presented. My facts are generally (or as we say in banking *directionally*) accurate, but I never made notes *that* good to remember every event or conversation verbatim. This is about finding your purpose, not any particular fact. I ask many questions. Do not copy or try to answer my specific questions – there are far too many for comfort. My questions aim to illustrate the need to dig deeper, not for you to answer what I present. Instead, I provide short end-of-chapter exercises to help you reflect on your life.

Please keep in mind that although I give you a lot of reasons not to do something, it doesn't mean you should not do it – just know why you're doing it. There are few universally bad choices (unless you're a criminal or your choices conflict with your values).

I hope to help veterans better frame their private sector experience, but this is not only for veterans. I wrote this book to help those wanting more from the private sector, veteran or not.

Lastly, you will find I contradict myself. Part of building a solid framework is acknowledging that things are not black and white. Your judgment will develop over time through experience and from the perspective imparted by this book, and you will find that nothing always works in every situation. I certainly do not have all the right answers, as the right answer often depends on values – yours and others. Simply thinking about problems before encountering them will help you navigate more effectively than flying blindly. By contradicting myself, I lead you into the grey to challenge my own points. The *right* thing is hardly ever straightforward, and the world is becoming more ambiguous every day.

Chapter 1:

Good Enough

My wife is a perfectionist. She's a straight-A student, valedictorian from high school, and an honors graduate from the U.S. Naval Academy and her medical school. When people ask me what I do for fun, I tell them I work. I love working. My favorite hobbies are my job, external learning, and remodeling my house (before having my daughter). But my wife is the hardest worker I know. She works too hard.

She was baffled by the concept of *good enough* when I first presented it to her. *Good enough* is incorporated throughout the other concepts in this book, and thus, it is the starting point. I love good enough.

Winston Churchill said, "Perfection is the enemy of progress."

Good enough is the **lack of perfection**.

Good enough **does not** mean poor quality.

I won't bore you with stories of the Big Tech giants who don't wait for perfection but continuously tinker with a good enough product – there are more than enough stories about them. I want to know how a lesson impacts me, not always some grand unrelatable tale, so I will try to provide something more tangible here.

After buying my house, I wanted to remodel my bathroom. I had never remodeled anything before. I watched many remodeling videos, talked to people with experience, and visited new housing developments to discover a sense of design and quality. Home builders are not perfectionists by any measure. Homes would cost far more if they were.

Home builders have a standard of quality. Exploring model homes will give you a sense of their standard – the models are far from perfect and represent the best the builder has to offer.

Most average-priced new homes have similar good enough quality standards, but there is variance between them. The quality improves with luxury homes – their good enough is better than the average. *Good enough* is not a static metric in any arena.

After I completed remodeling our bathroom, my wife inspected my work, detailing *all* of the imperfections. She suggested that we pay someone to remodel next time. I didn't argue. I took her to a million-dollar model home the following weekend and walked her through a bathroom. I pointed out all the same flaws she found in my work and explained the concept of acceptable variance. *Acceptable variance* is not intuitive to perfectionists.

Acceptable variance: the range of satisfactory quality. i.e., allowable imperfections.

Ch. 1 Good Enough

Manufacturers use the concept of acceptable variance in their processes because it is impossible to achieve a perfect output every time, but this does not mean they sell faulty products. Tradesmen also need to know what the standard is – what is good enough or what is acceptable variance in quality? Perfection takes too long for mass production and is impossible to achieve consistently. Poor quality is worse, and opportunities to sell low quality at a decent price are limited.

A tradesman who cannot meet the standard will finish one job and never receive a call-back. A developer incurs risks by hiring an untested tradesman because they do not know that person's standard. Trade unions ensure the quality is consistent, and developers understand the quality when they hire union. You don't become a master plumber in the union if you're not good enough. Say what you want about unions, but this is part of what makes them great – the quality standard.

Tradesmen will inevitably be asked to do more, not to take breaks, and/or ignore code at some point in their career. Some will abide because they have limited negotiating power and want to be called again. Union trades will not. They are the standard. A union's strength is in numbers (the aggregate group) and consistency (their good enough). The union allows workers to say no to unreasonable requests, such as violating building codes, to finish the job quickly. Unions take breaks and give the developer what they paid for. Unions do not give developers extra work for the same pay (i.e., a *good deal*). Perhaps consistency and, thus, less uncertainty, in hiring union workers can be more valuable than the potentially extra effort of a non-union tradesman.

Value is derived in various ways depending on what is desired – we'll develop this idea throughout the book. For now, let's consider a good enough consistent product to be the goal.

If you are like me or my family, you cannot work slowly. We are similar to non-union tradesmen being pressed for more and providing it. Johnsons complain about everyone else being lazy, but that's not true – we work harder because we do not understand the standard or what is good enough. If good enough entails working more slowly, we always give more than required. This is not a humble brag. Working harder than necessary is not a favorable trait in the private sector. The inevitable outcome of working harder is that we want and demand more from our employers who do not reward additional contributions (and your coworkers hate you for raising the bar). All an employer really wants is a good enough product or output, and for you to be content with your lot. My family is always unhappy in their jobs.

Know your employer's expectations – what do they want and at what quality? If you are self-employed, what is your standard? The U.S. Air Force taught me it is more desirable to be consistently okay than inconsistently great – customers need to know what they're getting from you. In finance, *risk* is defined as volatility, variability, and/or uncertainty. The more variable your output, the more risk you present, even at a higher quality. Your employer deducts the expected cost of the risk from your otherwise higher salary. Does getting more done come at the expense of consistency? For my family and many others, yes.

What does your spouse expect from you? This seems intuitive, but it isn't. Many people go years without knowing the standard and continuously give more and more. Some people are inconsistent, and their output is highly variable, even if sometimes great – their spouses and employers don't

Ch. 1 Good Enough

know what to expect from them. Others consistently underperform and are confused when they are let go from their job or their spouse leaves them

If married, you know the feeling of having an angry spouse who will not tell you what you did wrong but instead expects you to divine the knowledge. This is practice for identifying the standard elsewhere because it is up to you to figure it out. Very few people will tell you that you are underperforming in the private sector.

Nobody is going to tell you if you're overperforming, either. Ignore the risk of inconsistency for the moment. If you're an overperformer, what if the expectation is far less? What if the end user just wants the basics and doesn't see value in your extra effort? What if she just wants a McDouble, but you're giving her a Royale with Cheese for the same price?

Simply put, if McDonald's drenches their hamburger with ketchup, are you impressed by the extra effort? What if the employee likes it that way and thinks you would appreciate the same? Does that matter? She made the extra effort and spent more money on the inputs to each burger – you're still not impressed? No. And your employer is equally unimpressed with the extra effort (at least in terms of commensurate pay.)

McDonald's strength is in its consistency. McDonald's hardly has the best hamburger, but we continue to go there because it's familiar, consistent, and often good enough. It's certainly no Freddy's Steakburger, which is objectively good, always.

Back to the trades. I recently hired some tile guys to work on our house. The work required cutting back the carpet in the living room to expand our tiled steps. I recognize tile guys are not carpet experts. Their quote didn't include carpet work, and we never discussed it beyond cutting it back for the tile installation. I expected them to leave it when they were done – the tile was my primary focus. They were doing a fantastic job all week but fell behind on the last day. They appeared to be struggling a bit and eventually finished at 7 pm. They even reinstalled the carpet perfectly, or so it seemed.

Everything looked great on the surface, so they left. Upon closer inspection, I found that they installed the step's vertical face tile over the edge of the carpet to hold it down, but the carpet was pushing the tile up before the mortar dried. This was *unacceptable variance* and a tripping hazard for my pregnant wife. Most of it was an easy fix. I just pulled out the carpet and the tile set appropriately. But what if it went unnoticed? The tile would have set with a half-inch lip at the top. That is unacceptable. It's much harder and more expensive to fix something than to do it correctly the first time – this is why your dad was a dick about you making mistakes.

This company cut corners to complete more than the required work on time. Cutting corners is not good enough, and I lost respect for the company. Beyond that, adding value by "fixing" the carpet was not value-added because it detracted from their primary work – the tile, which they would have done a great job with if they weren't focused on something we never discussed. A simple question of "What should we do with the carpet?" would have solved this problem, and they would have completed it at a reasonable time. Instead, they never asked, worked late, and my wife and I wound up tired and stressed trying to figure out the problem at 9 pm on a Friday. No one was happy despite the extra effort.

Ch. 1 Good Enough

My DIY bathroom remodel cost less than $5,000 and included every tool required for the job (which I now own and can use on other projects). Contractors charge more than $20,000 for the same scope of work and similar quality. When I explained the cost savings to my wife, she said my work was…

Good enough.

Chapter Exercise: Perfection

Describe an endeavor in which you strived for perfection. Note if *good enough* could have sufficed. If so, quantify your additional effort in terms of what you didn't get to do instead.

1.

Could *good enough* suffice? (Y / N)

What did you give up to achieve perfection?

Chapter 2:

Source Data

In the first chapter, we learned that jobs have a *good enough* standard. The same is true for the sources of our opinions, life choices, investment decisions, and essentially everything else. What suffices as good enough for our endeavors may vary wildly, as does the amount of effort or research we put in to help guide our decisions. A good enough source for these items is achieved by balancing the cost and benefit of increased effort.

If you're buying a home, you may want to review the area's crime statistics, local home value trends, lenders, and mortgage terms. This is a big decision, so it's essential to do your due diligence, research extensively, and consider the best sources (e.g., local government statistics on crime vs. a top 10 best neighborhoods review, or working directly with a lender to discover your mortgage terms vs. Googling the question). A car is still a big decision, but you can get away with much less research than when buying a house. You probably don't think too hard about the potatoes you buy from the grocery store, nor should you. It's *small potatoes* if you will.

I'm sorry for the dad joke; I recently became a father. Please keep reading...

Sometimes, the required research is pre-defined by your industry, field, or subject. In accounting, the concept of *materiality* drives everything. Accounting provides financial information about a firm to ensure leaders can make decisions based on up-to-date data. Does the right decision require tracking a $5,000 transaction? It depends. If it's a mom-and-pop store, then it is probably material. If it is Apple Inc., perhaps not. In banking, we use materiality to define the information that would otherwise change our investment decision or terms. You can apply *materiality* to everyday life.

Materiality: an item that impacts your decision, if known.

What is *material* to the decision at hand?

Statistical analysis is a level of research we expect from some fields, while others may look at self-reported questionnaires or even reference fiction to make their case. Your domain and purpose will determine *materiality* and the quality of the research required.

Many of us have "researched" a sophisticated topic by surfing the internet. We look for news articles or websites that address our concerns. Even if mostly accurate, the provided information is prone to all the biases of their content creators, which impact the framing of the topic. Early in school, we learned that the news should provide who, what, when, where, how, and why; however, the news is becoming increasingly politicized and editorialized. Our news isn't just giving us the

Ch. 2 Source Data

facts; there is spin, opinion, and narrative that convolutes the message. This is often represented by "liberal" or "conservative" bias from certain sources, but it extends beyond that. Typically, you're reading an interpretation of data from an unsophisticated journalist. Are they representing it well?

Early in 2022, Vox put out a video titled *Why the US wants inflation, explained by fish*, and was one of many media sources framing high inflation as a favorable development. High inflation is objectively a bad thing. There is nothing more certain than the broad damaging impact of inflation. Who are these jabronis?

This is the problem with relying on tertiary or even lower-quality data. See, data goes through various filters before reaching the layman (us). Take economic data, for instance. The Federal Reserve compiles economic data. They share the raw data – *source data*, i.e., first order. They may even provide a simple narrative. Then, a media like Bloomberg, New York Times, or Reuters takes that information and writes their perspective on it – second or third order. Later, Fox News, CNN, Business Insider, or your local news station picks up the earlier article and adds their spin – this is often when the data is stripped entirely and replaced by a narrative of a narrative – third or worse order.

Source data: Information aggregated at the highest quality available.

Obviously, biases play a role, but you may not know the sophistication of the journalist. Can a journalist at Business Insider making $60,000 per year writing about the stock market really be 100% trusted while they (if qualified) could be making hundreds of thousands or even millions of dollars a year if they worked for a bank? I doubt it. It doesn't mean they're wrong. Just understand the quality of the source, the role the author's perspective and sophistication play in their writing, and the limitations of such.

Many lower-quality sources were acceptable throughout high school and potentially your undergrad. The expectations change as you develop professionally or progress into a graduate program. They won't want you to reference someone else's thoughts; they will expect you to look at *source data* and come to your own conclusions.

Very few undergraduate liberal arts programs require extensive source data analysis. Other programs that require comprehensive analysis tend to have the most job openings and the highest starting and mid-career salaries. An accountant uses source data to create a budget or prepare reports, a banker to make investment decisions, and an engineer to plan a project. Unsurprisingly, these are some of the highest-paying entry-level roles with great employment outlooks. Very few people outside of STEM fields know how to find or perceive relevant source data, even most business school graduates. Computer programmers and coders (many without degrees) create original work using quantifiable skills most people don't possess. Unsurprisingly, these jobs also all deal with numbers or logic. Math and source data are the difference between high and low-pay entry-level jobs. What is high pay? The fields referenced above commonly pay between $50,000 and $80,000 annually for new graduates with limited-to-no experience. Interns in these fields tend to out earn graduates from liberal arts programs, but it's not only about the money. *Source data* allows you to understand the world better.

Ch. 2 Source Data

I asked a former coworker what his wife did for work:

Coworker: "She's a doctor and owns a clinic."

Me: "Wow, what's her specialty?"

Coworker: "She's an MD."

Me: "I understand, but what's her specialty – family medicine, orthopedics, neurology?"

Coworker: "She's an ND."

I misheard him the first time when I heard "MD" and he was reluctant to make it clear,

Coworker: "Naturopathic doctor."

Me: ...

(I was confused and didn't quite know what that was.)

He went on about spending her free time "researching" the internet to find new naturopathic treatments and how insurance doesn't cover her treatments. I then realized what I was dealing with... The rigor is not even close to that of a standard medical doctor, and treatments are subject to the opinions of a single "doctor" without challenge.

Medical doctors (MDs) generally do not search the internet for new treatments. Ailments are typically well-known, identifiable, and with standard treatments available. There are accepted practices, and doctors conduct studies, develop, or dig into *source data* to better understand cutting-edge solutions. Most MDs are unwilling to experiment on everyday patients with an untested hypothesis. MDs receive a decision framework in medical school that is developed further in a multi-year residency. The rigor of naturopathic medicine is far from that of real medical doctors. This is why MDs make the big bucks, and insurance does not cover visits to the ND. It doesn't mean they're worthless, but extra skepticism of their opinion is warranted. Listening to them uncritically is like making an investment decision based on a Business Insider article.

The more sophisticated a subject, the more prone we are to using third (or worse) order information as laymen. This happens a lot with climate research. Despite being a "settled" science among the *educated*, most of us have never read a climate study. We rely on an unspecialized journalist, activist, or politician to tell us what the studies say, yet we are adamant that we understand the problem.

Further, news stories about studies rarely give us the details and use sensationalized descriptions. Vox reported that a PLOS One analysis found that only 48.7% of 156 studies reported by newspapers were confirmed in subsequent reviews. Conclusions of more than half of the reported studies could not be verified! (If you're concerned about the irony of me relying on a report of a study to tell you not to trust reports of studies... you're just going to have to deal with it – it was *good enough* to make my point).

Some academic journals of less-sciency *sciences* have been found to accept politicized topics without regard to substance – especially in the social sciences. Take the academic journal Cogent Social Science's acceptance of the phony article *The Conceptual Penis as a Social Structure*. The hoaxers used a compelling title with a nonsense narrative to test the quality of the journal's review. The journal failed miserably by publishing a fraudulent work that contained no value. The ridiculousness of the article title is matched only by its authentic appearance, given gender studies ideology. But that's all it takes to be published in that field – use the right-sounding phrases and buzzwords. This doesn't mean the information from these sources or academic journals is valueless (excluding this specific article) – just be aware of the potentially low quality of information presented.

Given the apparent flaw in peer review here, did the leaders of these fields make a name for themselves by producing similarly fraudulent works? Think of the quality of education you receive if you choose to study these topics (even when it is more *sciency* sounding, like naturopathic medicine).

Dr. Eric Stewart, PhD, a professor of Criminology at Florida State University, was fired from the school in 2023 after several of his studies were retracted. Neither the data nor the conclusions supporting his claims of racism in the American criminal justice system could be corroborated – but what an intriguing narrative he helped develope! Reversing the impact of racism is a prevalent agenda of the current social justice era, and racism in the criminal justice system is believable to most *educated* people given the extensive "research" on the topic – probably why he got away with it for nearly 15 years. In 2019, a fellow researcher disputed his conclusions from a joint study and claimed Mr. Stewart falsified data (does he really deserve the "Dr." title?). This prompted additional scrutiny, and now, six of his studies have been retracted in just a few years.

The university initially "investigated" the claims but had two of Mr. Stewart's other co-researchers on their three-person inquiry committee (conflict of interest?), never requested the original data, and unsurprisingly found no evidence to support a further investigation, and the case was closed without reprimand. That is until another study was retracted, and additional data falsification claims arose from other researchers. The university could no longer ignore the issue and opened an actual investigation this time around.

Although FSU did not validate claims of falsification when they finalized their latest investigation, their review was sufficient to support firing him. At best, their actions mean that they could not corroborate his data and/or conclusions on numerous studies. At worst, they found falsification but were unwilling to say so publicly. The failure to validate falsification claims certainly does not disprove them. Given the allegations and the lack of supporting data, it is likely that he falsified his analysis. How do we know other *leaders* in this field are more rigorous in their research if certain narratives are incentivized (think of the consulting opportunities or potential book deals on *anti-racism* in the modern era), and peer review doesn't occur until *repeated* misconduct claims arise?

Oh yeah, that's what Mr. Stewart's critic and original whistle-blower, Professor Justin Pickett, Ph.D., said "There's a huge monetary incentive to falsify data and there's no accountability. If you do this, the probability you'll get caught is so, so low." Dr. Pickett's article titled *How Universities Cover up Scientific Fraud* provides key details on how to conduct an investigation if you do not desire an adverse outcome. Essentially, just do everything FSU did – task people with conflicts of interest (coauthors who may have their own studies questioned from an adverse conclusion), never request information that could prove fraud (the data), and only interview the person accused while giving them 100% of the benefit of the doubt. I would not be surprised to find a Vox article justifying the falsification of data if it supports a good cause, given their stance on inflation. Oh, the social *sciences*...

Speaking of naïve young adults being taken advantage of... the media builds narratives about society to motivate you to act. One article from 2022 is about a millennial who built a passive income empire using Airbnb. It discusses her project, how she got started, her minimal investment, and how much she makes, and only if you read the entire article do you find out **she inherited a large chunk of land in Hawaii near a volcano and national park**. Hmmm... do you think inheriting valuable property may have something to do with her success in real estate? Why not skip the B.S. and simply write an article titled *I won the lottery, and so can you!*

Another article details an investor in Florida who bought a $2 million condo and *passively* earns a *pitiful* (my word, not theirs) $3,000 per year on it. He invested millions and only makes a few thousand per year? Who is this jabroni? $3,000 / $2,000,000 = 0.15%. Not 15%. Less than a 1% annual return and probably the worst investment I have ever heard someone brag about. *But it's passive.* Gross. Go buy a lottery ticket and keep waiting for the world to hand you everything you ever wanted.

Why would they promote that narrative? Because many people are lazy and never do the math (fitting for those dreaming of *passive* income). The journalist is probably equally unsophisticated and never checked the return. They also may be receiving a payoff to promote these narratives. There are infinite reasons someone may be bad at their job (or corrupt). It's up to you to check their work when driven to action.

A condo development in Minneapolis, Minnesota, marketed toward *passive* investors looking to rent them short-term (Airbnb-style) originally listed its units for sale at vastly inflated prices. They also provided a return calculator based on their expectations. They expected investors to earn a $3,000 per year profit on a $300,000 to $600,000 investment = less than a 1% annual return. A dog-shit return, no doubt, although much better than the jabroni in Florida. Most of their assumptions appeared appropriate; however, I almost missed their assumption for labor to maintain the apartment.

$9 per hour estimated. Minimum wage is $15 per hour in Minneapolis.

The return declined far below $0 when you adjust their labor estimate for minimum wage (assuming you can find someone to work that cheaply) – investors are losing money every year.

Who cares about wage costs, right? Investors can clean the apartment and manage it themselves to increase returns. OK. That can maximize returns on the rents; however, the investors are then working for less than minimum wage, and it's no longer passive. Is this the best use of their time? (They have the funds to invest over $300K-plus but are willing to work for $9 per hour equivalent?)

Or, leverage will maximize returns – $30K down (10%), and the rest borrowed increases investors' potential gains. However, cash flow is still negative, and they now have a mortgage to repay.

Or, let's say investors aren't holding units for the rents; they buy for the capital gains. Great. Please tell me what gains are expected on a property that is purchased expecting a return but now provably loses money each year. **It's nil**. Nada. Zilch. If you buy a condo at $300,000 expecting a 1% return each year (base case by the developer), but the market shifted, and you now lose 5% each year, the condo is worth less today than when you bought it – there are only capital **losses**. Otherwise, you're looking for a *good deal*, a sucker to take this off your hands at a higher valuation. Are you scheming? Quit scheming and just buy a lottery ticket.

Actually, scratch that – I've got a great investment opportunity for you!

That was in 2019, and the eight total Google reviews (all one-star ratings) at the time of this writing do not tell a favorable story. Presumably, the lousy cash flow has left management with no choice but to cut costs and reduce quality, resulting in terrible reviews. How has the broader Downtown Minneapolis market performed in the last four years? Objectively terribly. Here is a sample condo for sale as of the time of this chapter's first draft (February 2023, per Zillow.com).

Unit Description: Two bedroom, Two bath, 1,333 sq ft., 15th floor.

Previously Sold Date and Price: 5/11/2020, $510,000.

Most Recent List Date and Current Asking Price: 6/24/2021, $479,000 (-$70,900 from the seller's original listing price of $549,900. And yes, listed for over a year and a half and several months before the rising rate environment).

Original Sold Date and Price: 6/14/2018, $557,438.

Before the unit sold in 2020, that seller had it listed for almost a year.

This is a lovely condo built in 2018, and it's representative of the middle-to-high-end units in the area. Most other units for sale are facing an equally challenging environment.

So what happened?

The local market peaked around 2018/2019, and each buyer of the above unit subsequently lost money on the sale. It lost nearly 9% of its value between 2018 and 2020 and at least another 6% since (although still not selling, with a more significant loss likely to be realized). The area also missed out on the tremendous COVID real estate boom that led to skyrocketing values in most of the country – exacerbating the *opportunity cost* of investing here up to another 40%-plus during the three years.[1]

Why is Minneapolis in decline? The real estate market there boomed from 2016 to 2018, partly in anticipation of the 2019 Super Bowl. Local news consistently ran stories about increased property values and anticipated short-term rental costs (AirBnB) ahead of the big game. Investors snatched up real estate thinking they could chuck a few bucks into a property and rent it out for thousands or tens of thousands of dollars per night, then flip it afterward for massive profits. These rental rates largely never materialized. Later, local news highlighted investors who couldn't rent their property during the game (probably linked to the high nightly charges). It was also Minneapolis in February.

Minneapolis also had strict COVID policies prolonging closures and mandates and massively increasing crime in previously business-forward areas. Readily available city crime data tells us that reported crime only increased by 14% from 2019 to 2020, but a closer inspection tells a more concerning story. Arson (+66%), gunshot wound victims (+96%), homicide (+76%), shots fired (+120%), and weapons law violations (+28%) all increased significantly. Does the decline

---

[1] Post-edit update: the above unit later sold for $450,000, a $60,000 cost-basis loss.

in crimes like counterfeiting/forgery (-40%), drug/narcotic offenses (-38%), and embezzlement (-82%) make you feel safer? Probably not. Chances are the non-violent crimes didn't actually decline; only their reporting fell because residents had more concerning matters. Qualitatively, the situation is even more dire given that Minnesota locked down tightly at the onset of COVID with fewer opportunities for violent crime to occur. Tens of thousands of daily downtown workers stayed home in the suburbs, and the city shut down restaurant dining and bars for nine months of the year.

Politicians and real estate investors in the city tell us all is well because the crime growth rates are slowing dramatically. This is the equivalent of them telling us that slowing inflation solves the problem – it does not. Crime is still at very high levels, and slowing inflation doesn't make my baby's diapers any cheaper – we're still stuck with record-high crime and prices as the new normal.

Additionally, Minnesota had a net outflow of residents after COVID that adversely impacted demographics (not surprising with those crime rates in their largest city). Local politicians have done little to ease the pain. A different 350+ unit apartment building in Minneapolis was built in 2014 for $118 million and sold for $74 million in 2023 – a 37% cost-basis loss. The Downtown Minneapolis Hilton (the largest hotel in the area with over 800 units) also foreclosed in 2023. If Hilton cannot survive, how do you think the individual short-term rental market is doing?

I am not prescribing investment advice here except to **know what you are buying**. Jumping into an investment because of a series of articles or influencers portraying how easy it is and how everyone else is becoming wealthy, but you're not (FOMO), and you'll get burned. Dig for source data and come to your own conclusions as best you can in order to build a *sustainable* life.

Nassim Nicholas Taleb's best-selling book *Antifragile* discusses probability theory, risk, uncertainty, and most importantly, the idea that time destroys the fragile. The real estate narratives I described above are fragile. I will provide many more examples in which popular narratives work for a short period but never last long – i.e., they are fragile. My goal is to help you build on sustained and replicable performance and inspire you to be *antifragile*.

Pro-tip: Inherit a bunch of land in Hawaii to start off your real estate empire. I'll take my job at Business Insider now, please.

Ch. 2 Source Data

Chapter Exercise 1: Information Sources

List the last three sources from which you received information (news, website, your conspiracy-theory-obsessed buddy, Mel Gibson).

1.

2.

3.

Are they trying to sell you something and/or motivating you to act? (Y / N)

Does the narrative sound too good to be true? (Y / N)

Chapter 3:

Value

Finance is the study of value. Specifically, finance is the study of relative and expected economic value. Generally, we can consider value (non-financial) to be what is important to us. *Axiology* is the generalized study of value and the primary focus of this chapter.

Value is the foundation of your being. It is the what, who, when, where, how, and why. What do you do? With whom do you do it? When do you do it? Where do you do it? How do you do it? Why do you do it?

Minimal personal progress is achievable without knowing in which direction to go. A shotgun approach to life and activities can build perspective, but working hard and getting nowhere is discouraging – I was stuck here, and millions of other people have been, too. Values help find *it*.

What is *it*? That's what we're here to discover. Your *it* depends on what you value. Do you want money, time,

Ch. 3 Value

power, fame, happiness, friendships, possessions, or whatever? Those are decent starting points, but we will discuss how to dig deeper into why you want things such as money – money for money's sake is useless. Money is a tool to buy products, services, experiences, change, or power. Why do you want your *it*, and how do you obtain *it*?

Value identification is separate from intelligence. You could be brilliant but have no idea what is of value and lack intelligence but understand what is of value. Understanding what is of value to yourself **and** others is the starting point for building *the good life* – no intelligence required.

Let's start with what other people want. You can apply this concept to virtually everything – relationships, business, work, hobbies, and more. As to not make this about money, why do your friends like you? Are you funny, adventurous, curious, interesting, or a pushover? There are 8 billion people in the world; there must be a reason your friends like *you*.

I had a friend from high school who was rather annoying. He was obnoxious, rowdy, and lacking in character, but he was hilarious and he pushed me to become a better skateboarder. While I generally don't appreciate annoying people, his favorable characteristics compensated for the unfavorable ones.

He provided a great time through high school and in our twenties. I enjoyed being around someone interesting. Into our thirties, this friend's annoying characteristics started to outweigh the comedy. Did he do anything differently? No, and that was my problem. Getting kicked out of a bar in our thirties, hitting on random women, and pissing all over the bathroom floor is just plain embarrassing. I am sure he is the same at nearly 40 years old.

My values changed. I stopped valuing comedy as much as I valued stability. My life would be filled with troublemaker friends like him if my values never changed.

If you do not know why you associate with your friends or partner, I encourage you to consider this. Being lonely is a reason to have unexamined friends, but is it a good one? Your partner has sex with you, but is it meaningful, and do you jive? I've been in both of these scenarios. Never having a strong partner, I accepted the bare minimum. I never thought true happiness could be found with someone because everyone I knew had many of the same problems with their partners – I was wrong because my value framework was flawed. My *forever wife* is the greatest inspiration in my life. What does this have to do with the private sector? Everything. Neither your job nor your business exists in a vacuum. Bear with me.

It is worth a try to be purposeful in your associations. Aligning with people extends beyond political views or personalities. Alignment needs to encompass who you are, where you are, what you want, where you want to be, and with whom you want to do it – i.e., your *values*. But this is just the description from 30,000 feet.

Examining why you think people associate with you is a necessary endeavor. You're not the hot shit you think you are. You have many bad qualities, just like my rowdy friend, but people appreciate you because your favorable characteristics make up the difference – for now. I am no different. The popular Pearl Jam song *Elderly Woman Behind the Counter* lyrics, "I changed by not changing at all" are a critical statement to learn from. Are you keeping up with time?

If your parents pushed you to go to college or your grandparents pressed you to save your money, there is a reason for this – it should make life easier in the long run. But, planning and investing takes a lot of upfront effort, and it must be a conscious decision. Investing doesn't need to be monetary, either. It just requires taking from today for the benefit of tomorrow (education). Planning requires an understanding of your values so that you may invest effectively.

Value → Plan → Invest

Below, we will consider planning with investment as "Progression" and lack of planning and inaction as "Stagnation." Progression starts hard and becomes incrementally easier. Stagnation starts easy and becomes incrementally harder. Planning is a thought process. Investment is the action required to create anything meaningful from the plan. Again, this doesn't need to be about money. Here is a sample future for a 20-year-old:

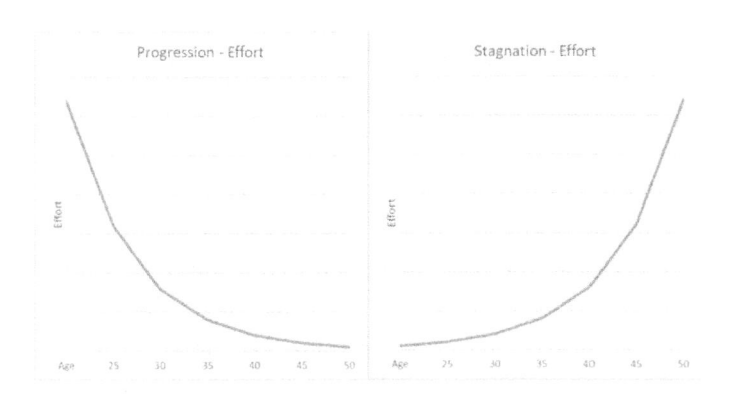

While there is no numerical value for "Effort," and it is used solely to represent the concept, we see that life becomes exponentially more difficult if you fail to plan and invest. Conscious progression provides the opposite.

Many professional certifications require continuing education credits. Becoming a CPA is already a challenging endeavor. Still, you cannot pass the CPA exam one time and never learn again – a CPA is required to continuously learn to maintain their certification. This is so they *do not change by not changing*. But education is also exponentially easier with experience, and the burden of studying is relieved over time even if the number of required classes does not. Effort declines while a CPA's pay steadily rises.

Life-long learning is a requirement not just for progression but also for maintaining. People have more energy in their youth. Looking at the Stagnation graph: will you keep up when the required effort increases substantially around 45-50 years of age? The concept is labeled "Stagnation" because you are not changing, but it should not be interpreted as implying a flat or stable outcome – the failure to act makes life more difficult over time, as we see with the Effort axis.

If you're a carpenter working 60 hours a week at 30 years old to afford your debts and lifestyle, can you sustain those hours when you're 50? If not, your earnings will decline significantly, and your lifestyle will rapidly deteriorate. The effort to maintain your income will increase even if the hours worked do not – physical labor will become more demanding over time. Hopefully, you're managing jobs or performing quality control of other people's work by this time or have saved enough money to lighten your workload and not be impacted. Transitioning out of direct day-to-day labor and affording the same lifestyle requires planning and investing in developing new skills (education) or a substantial nest egg (financial investment). If you can maintain the overtime, good for you. Or is this just a problem for *future-you* to worry about?

Worse yet, if you're clubbing at 30 years old and spend your money, time, and energy picking up women at the bar and not into developing strong relationship skills, how hard will it be to pick up chicks at 45 or 50 when you're old, out of shape, and haggard? The required money, time, or energy will increase drastically in that endeavor as you become less desirable to the younger crowd as the creepy old dude.

Planning and investing are necessary for your long-term well-being and obtaining what you want, regardless of what that is. Value identification is the starting point.

If you want to work on Wall Street, do you just roll the dice and apply? Hopefully not. Job descriptions, requirements, and a company's *About Us* page help identify what they value – just this component takes a lot of time to review. Then, assess your position and build experience based on your findings. Job requirements are the *Quantitative* values – number of years of experience, number of projects, the degree. The *Qualitative* values are what they may not put in the description – the company wants Harvard graduates, Fortune 500 company experience, someone who will work 100-hour weeks, or a call from your dad who is CEO at another company. These are actual requirements at some firms, but they will rarely say them out loud.

This is what they value.

So, what do you value?

Let's differentiate between facts and values. There are *facts*: The U.S. is a country with over 300 million people. Then there are *values*: freedom or helping society's most vulnerable. Values are kind of like opinions, but they should drive you to action – e.g., join the military or lobby for improved public programs.

Ch. 3 Value

I don't love the idea of thinking of grand themes for values – Freedom, God, Country – because they're very abstract. They're an acceptable starting point, but you need to dig deeper. If you identify freedom as a value, do you mean 100% freedom, no laws or restrictions (i.e., anarchy)? People mean different things with these terms, so I advise thinking less on the macro and more in the micro about this.

Freedom may mean having time to do the things you enjoy, choosing your job, or spending time with family. Perhaps it means owning land and having a space of your own. It may mean owning nothing and having nothing tying you down. These are very different concepts of freedom. If you value helping society's vulnerable, you must dig deeper to define what programs or how you want to help people – does providing sterile needles and other paraphernalia help drug addicts, or does tough love, enforcing laws, and making arrests set them on the course for correction? Is correcting their drug addiction the goal, or is the goal to make their addiction safer without minimizing usage? What you mean depends on you. Values are not just words ("helping"). Values are concepts, and they must be specific to be meaningful.

Values can be conceptualized simply as: if you could snap your fingers to have what you want, what would you choose? You must be specific. The 2000 film *Bedazzled*, starring Brendan Fraser and Elizabeth Hurley, illustrates my point perfectly. Elizabeth Hurley plays the Devil and grants Brendan Fraser's character wishes in exchange for his soul. But the wishes never come out as expected because each has a tradeoff, and he isn't specific enough. His wish to be rich and powerful makes him a Columbian Drug Lord with law enforcement on his trail. This is far from what he envisioned as being rich and powerful. The Devil is in the details.

Ch. 3 Value

Values answer the question of "what matters most?" and help prioritize your actions.

Does everything matter equally?

In his *Great Courses* lectures on value, Professor Patrick Grim shares a tale of a lunatic escaping from an insane asylum. The lunatic knows he is insane. His strategy for appearing sane in public involves only saying the facts, as how can facts be wrong? Well, his lunacy is easily discovered. Walking down the street, he states, "There are cracks in the sidewalk. There's a cat on that wall." While absolutely true, very few sane people would find these facts important enough to proclaim, and so he is caught. He couldn't differentiate between the importance of minutia and the rest of the world. **He didn't know what to value, so *anything* became important** despite having a solid handling of the facts. Facts are easy and indisputable. It's not a lack of facts, but a lack of values explains why we spend hours each day playing video games, watching TV, and obtaining college degrees that provide no skills, or worse yet, sitting at our dead-end job surfing social media all day.

Values give us purpose, the ability to self-actualize, and/or help others with such. Think of an artist who knows her craft, works hard on it day after day, and sells her work to willing buyers who enjoy it and the fulfillment provided by that appreciation. That requires a particular set of values.

Imagine how disappointing the world would be if you walked down a path and couldn't see a difference in value between the beauty of the mountains on one side, the sun setting over the ocean on the other, and a crack in the sidewalk, or an ant. You would be of little value working in real estate.

Furthermore, you cannot discern values or what you ought

to do from facts alone (called the *is-ought gap*) – you need a framework. You can read the Bible cover-to-cover, be able to recite each passage from memory, and still not know why "Thou shalt not kill" is important. Only the value placed on the respect of other people, their families, an orderly society, and/or the God who commands it gives it meaning. As universal as *not killing* should be, a lot of it occurs, illustrating that people have different or competing values. A values framework explains why you can be atheist or agnostic and still have morals or believe the Ten Commandments are a net positive for the world – God was only one of the values presented in my list.

Values don't need to be profound.

Financial analysis involves taking facts and converting them into values. In banking, we look at a company, we state a bunch of facts, and we then make a jump from the facts to values – "The company is growing revenue rapidly (fact), and therefore we should invest (value)." We cannot discern whether or not to invest just by stating facts about the company. Two investors can come to different conclusions based on their values (perhaps one's value is the bonus received for such a recommendation, and the other is an old curmudgeon who rarely likes any companies and may or may not be this author…).

Finance does not only teach how to value an asset; it provides a framework for a relative assessment. Imagine a manager selecting one of two possible projects. How do they know which one to choose if both projects share the same expected value or return? Financial theory provides a correct answer. That is the power of a framework.

Ch. 3 Value

I work as an Examiner (i.e., analyst or risk manager) in Corporate and Investment Banking, which requires understanding what information (facts) matters (values). This is one of the hardest things for an analyst to decipher. An inexperienced analyst's report is always much longer than it needs to be. Young analysts include *everything* about a company or deal because they rarely know what is important. They point out the cracks in the sidewalk and cats on the wall.

Analysts receive guidance from loan approvers who tend to have extensive experience. There is hardly any consistency, even among experienced loan approvers. Some want more detail than others. Some understand the gist and are OK with it. Others will lean on the analyst to tell them what's important if they aren't familiar with the industry. Not everyone values the same information. This inconsistency makes it even harder for analysts to learn what matters. Knowing what matters (what to value) is the difference between a commercial loan analyst making $70,000 and
$250,000+ per year for essentially the same job. Suppose the Approver (also a very well-paid position) can adjudicate twice as many loans because the bank has a staff of experienced analysts. That is valuable to the company and, therefore, the higher pay for all.

Some banks don't truly want their analysts to analyze. They use technical jargon, graphs, and projections to make it appear their employees did their due diligence to process as many loans as possible. So, it may even be that the organization values people who are bad at their jobs as analysts/risk managers. These banks use the risk management function to fool regulators into believing due diligence occurs and that there is a separation of duties and incentives for sales and risk employees – but there isn't. All they want is to originate loans as quickly as possible by stating facts without using any judgement. This is what they value.

You must know what your employer values. They'll give you part of that picture, but as I said earlier, they will never say everything they want out loud.

Student loan servicing companies were accused of acting in bad faith by providing adverse incentives to their representatives. Managers monitored employees' time with each customer, incentivizing shorter calls rather than taking the time to help. The representatives gave insufficient and misleading information to those applying for Public Service Loan Forgiveness (PSLF), and thousands of borrowers never obtained the benefits they were entitled to due to such recklessness. According to NPR, 99% of PSLF applications had been denied by 2019, the year after tens of thousands of borrowers became eligible. The borrowers were real people who made the right decisions and did what they were told to do, and they got screwed. There was no incentive for the servicing representatives to help borrowers – their companies valued the enhanced profitability of hiring fewer employees and having each handle more calls (and therefore allotting less time to help each borrower). The government agency that contracted with these entities made no attempt to ensure they were operating appropriately. I doubt the companies ever told the representatives to give out false information; they just created an environment that incentivized the behavior they desired (less time per call) and saved money on reduced staffing and inadequate training – the rest followed.

Political ideologues often tell me that if I only knew what they know, I would agree. It's not about the facts; it's about values.

Ch. 3 Value

After the 2020 Presidential election, the political Right had wild conspiracies about why President Donald Trump lost the election. Talk of a conspiracy with Cuba interfering with voting machines turned most people off because it is not 1960. The stories were extensive, convoluted, and unbelievable to most Americans. Except for ballot harvesting. We know ballot harvesting occurred. Combined with very rapidly implemented unconstitutional changes to election procedures, it is *very* possible enough ballots were harvested to sway the elections in battleground states. Team Trump had statistics on their side, but the convoluted narrative sounded too conspiratorial for the average American. Could his team stick to one point and drive it home? Absolutely not. They had to fight every battle regardless of the severity or quality of evidence. They may have made progress if they stuck to a single believable narrative. Instead of picking their battles, they fought them all and lost. In a very Trump-like manner, he valued calling out *every* perceived injustice.

The political Left moves mountains because they know what points to make and when. "Peaceful Protest" was reiterated over and over again on the news during the George Floyd/Black Lives Matter riots, *eh hem*, peaceful protests of 2020, even as the reporter stood in front of a burning building. The Left chooses a phrase or word to represent their entire message – "peaceful protest" regarding the George Floyd riots and "insurrection" regarding the January 6th protests. As rioters burned down or looted entire city blocks and filmed it, most news sources told you it was a "peaceful protest." No garbled or convoluted conspiracy. You could see it with your own eyes, but they stuck to the phrase – the simple narrative – regardless of the situation. The Left picks a point, and *everyone* drives it home.

The Left doesn't care if they are accurate as long as they convey their message, and their results speak volumes. This is a matter of values.

The Walt Disney Co. (and other film companies) pander to the Chinese Communist Party's demands for their movies. Disney or others must abide if they want to distribute their films in China. This amounts to a foreign government demanding censorship here in the U.S. as producers alter films viewed domestically at the discretion of the CCP overseas. Most *known* influences involve how Chinese-related countries or people are represented and appear relatively harmless. The direct relationship to items is only known due to watchful sleuths checking the background. It may involve the removal of Taiwan from the map or the Taiwanese flag from the flight suit of a Navy fighter pilot. It may be more insidious, but that hasn't been proven yet. Disney *et al.* are not disclosing the censorship they've agreed to.

In the credits to Disney's *Mulan*, eight Chinese government entities tied to the Xinjiang region, where China uses Uighur slave labor, are thanked. What did these government entities and police forces do for Disney? Not sure, but it implies Disney worked closely with them. One would expect a woke company to care about slavery. Interestingly, they don't.

Alternatively, in America, Disney went head-to-head with Florida Governor Ron DeSantis. DeSantis signed new legislation that banned the instruction of sexual preference and identity to children younger than fourth grade, dubbed "Don't Say Gay" by his critics. Disney condemned the legislation and vowed to help repeal it. They appeased slaveholders and the Chinese Communist Party but openly fought with an extremely popular U.S. politician and vowed to involve themselves in local politics. This illustrates Disney's values.

You may be similar to the earlier discussed escaped lunatic, but perhaps not as extreme. You may think little about cracks in a sidewalk, but what would you find if you examined how you spend your time and energy, or more simply, what you talk about? Your thoughts are like real estate: space is limited, so make good use of it. The pages of this book are the same – there is a limit to what I can fit. Why did I choose my examples? My examples illustrate my values.

Everyone has the same number of hours in a day, but how are some people more productive? Or, how are some people more effective in obtaining what they want or getting to where they want to be?

I had another friend in high school who became my mentor (yes, a mentor can be someone your age). This friend had many disadvantages – a brain tumor in his mid-teens, divorced parents, a distant father, a very working-class upbringing, and he came from a "white-trash" family by any objective measure. He also insisted he was not very smart. He became a *six-figure earner* before his thirties without a college degree and was consistently the highest earner in our friend group until recently. During our senior year in high school and for the next few years, he spent his nights and weekends building IT servers in his mom's basement. While other friends were going out and cruising around, he spent his time at home working because he valued professional progression more than having a good time. We made fun of him until we realized that he had the juice and we didn't. He wasn't handed an opportunity. He found what he wanted (valued), worked on it, sacrificed, and eventually got paid well for his expertise. He was also a virgin far longer than the other friends.

We'll talk about tradeoffs later.

He tried to convince me to specialize and focus on a single goal. I didn't know what to do, so I took a shotgun approach. I got a little bit of experience in many areas and jumped around. I disliked most of my choices. I made very little progress in anything after years of action. In college, I continued to take easy classes that taught me nothing except how to fool the professor into giving me an "A" – which is relatively easy when you're moderately informed and the class takes no skill.[2]

Define what you want. This is no easy task.

Defining what you want in detail takes time and effort. You must break through the general (money, time, a hot partner, more books from this author...). There are several layers of why you need to work through. Whatever you want, ask: **why do you want it, and at what cost?** Think of yourself as a three-year-old – why, why, why?

Let's deconstruct a man's common goal.

Example Goal: "To make a six-figure salary."

Why: "To make money to buy things. Women like men who make lots of money. Security."

Constraints: "Currently making $40,000/year. Time. Lack of tangible skills."

---

[2] Side note: beware of easy courses, even as electives; your laziness will be well communicated to prospective employers. Guess how many people are impressed by "Peace Ethics" on my transcript? If you guessed none, you're giving me too much credit – this class detracts value for its ridiculousness

Ch. 3 Value

Dig deeper into the *Why?*

Why do you want to buy more things, or what do you want to buy? What kind of women look for men who make lots of money – are they the kind of partner you want? What type of security are you looking for? Why can't you have security without a six-figure salary? Why are you only making $40,000 vs. $100,000+ right now? This is just a sample of the necessary questions; you must be brutally honest in your answers. Are you just keeping up with the Joneses?

The *Hedonic Treadmill* is the concept that our tastes progress as we achieve our goals. You make $40,000 per year now and want things someone making $50,000 or $60,000 has. When you make more money, you'll always desire the next best thing out of reach. So, once you make a six-figure salary, will you just want six figures plus more and perpetually stew in your own unsatisfaction? I love progress and money, so I chose to be perpetually unsatisfied – it's OK.

An example values-discovery is below:

What do you want: "Money."

Why: "To buy a sports car to go out in."

Why: "To impress women and hook up."

Why: "To impress my friends."

There is no helping you if you're this shallow. Dig deeper. Alternatively (and preferably):

What do you want: "Money."

Ch. 3 Value

Why: "To buy a house, save for retirement, give my kids the opportunities I didn't have."

How much money does that take: "About $100,000 per year."

Why do you want to buy vs. rent a home: "Buying provides the ability to make the home my own and I want stability."

Why do you need to make more to achieve this: "My goal is to retire by 60. Inflation has already stretched our family too thin. Without higher income, we must cut back on retirement savings that will delay retirement, we may not be able to afford to buy a home, and our kids won't be able to play hockey like I did at their age."

What are you willing to give up to support the extensive earnings and savings this will require: "We are attending night school to build new skills and will buy a fixer-upper rather than a new build."

Fair enough. This conversation could go an infinite number of ways, and we could dig much deeper, but it should give you an idea, as the protagonist, of the necessary time required to consider your options. This example person had to work out a budget, project for retirement, and explore career opportunities to understand what is required – and their work is incomplete. They may not even have a good plan and be wrong about their projections, but they're thinking about it. The more effort you put into the plan and defining your it, the better it will be, and the more likely you will achieve *it*.

Specialists are available to help you for a small fee if you're concerned about the detail or sophistication required for your plan.

Ch. 3 Value

I don't live on a strict budget, but I find it helpful to check my bank account and track my transactions over the last few months occasionally. This tells me what I value, financially speaking. I often disappoint myself and use this experience to make more conscious spending decisions. Did I really value fast food five times last month? Yes, I did, and I won't change that. Mmmm Juliobertos California burritos...

A friend once commented that he planned to buy $1 million in real estate, stop working, and live off the rent. First, that is not a plan. That is a goal. Second, the plan is the most challenging part – how do you obtain the million dollars to buy the real estate? This was his near-term goal, but he made $40,000 per year. It will take him 25 years just to earn a million dollars on a pre-tax basis.

After taxes, it could take him 10 to 20-plus years to save enough just for a standard down payment on that much property. Not only did he skip the hardest part – how to get the million dollars – he never even did the math, as easy as it was, to see this is a very **long-term** goal. Additionally, he failed to account for the loan debt service if he planned to use debt. This will eat away his cash flow, and it will be insufficient to live on until the loans are fully repaid 20+ years after purchase. Perhaps he is a trust-fund baby and not investing with his earned income. I'm not sure. Doesn't matter. Let's look at this example:

Real Estate Value: $1,000,000.

Down Payment: $200,000.

Mortgage: $800,000.

Term: 25 years.

Annual Interest Rate: 6%.

Monthly Loan Payment: $5,150.

Monthly Property Tax and Insurance: $1,300 (estimated).

Rent required to break even: **$6,450 per month** = $5,150 + $1,300.

Market rent on a $1 million property (as researched on 2/22/2023): **$5,000 per month**[3].

Cash inflow of $5,000 minus Cash outflow of $6,450 = -$1,450 per month. A sizeable monthly cash shortfall.[4]

Long-term goals are great, but you need to recognize them as such so you don't leap into a situation quickly. Rash decisions can result in discouragement because you don't quickly achieve what you intended and end up switching goals again. Or, you are forced to keep your day job and work a second job to meet the reinvestment needs of the property because you jumped into an opportunity without thinking through the nuance.

---

[3] The rent used here was the last asking rent on a property for sale for $950,000 in zip code 55401 without a meaningful HOA fee. Such fee would increase ownership costs and rental income. I selected the property due to its proximity to my friend, and it was the closest listing price to my example size with a recent market-rate rental listing. The $50,000 difference in value is not material to our analysis, nor is a 30-year loan vs. the 25-year presented. A 20-year mortgage is probably even more typical for investors, weakening the case for a small-time investor further.

[4] There are potentially favorable tax implications to include in a formal analysis and this is only meant to illustrate the absurdity of the idea that this would change his life. Combining all items (tax deductions, management expenses, vacancy, repairs, etc.) and the simplified analysis above is moderately pessimistic. However, the result is still the same – the cash flow is insufficient for anyone to live on. I hope he keeps his day job to make up the difference because the income will not cover the costs in the short run.

Ch. 3 Value

This is a real goal for this 30-year-old, and it's commonly shared among young adults. *If only I had $1 million, I could do everything I dreamed of.* Except you can't because you don't know how to plan. But that is why we're working on it – let's get you there.

In *Antifragile*, Nassim Nicholas Taleb argues that stresses are required to build sustainability. Weak systems avoid stresses and arbitrarily advance in leaps rather than incrementally progressing into the type of system desired. Systems are strengthened by moderate stresses earned with more experience. These stresses are required to develop resiliency (or antifragility). Suppose you were gifted a million dollars without having gone through the struggles of working, earning, saving, and investing the funds over time. How would you know what a good investment looks like?

Part of understanding the quality of an investment is to consider its *opportunity cost*. The above million-dollar property pays $60,000 per year **gross**. That does not consider debt service, maintenance costs, updates, damages, defaulting tenants, and all the other items that can go wrong. If you had $1 million invested in 6% corporate bonds, they could provide the same cash flow opportunity at lower risk. You may also invest the million in an S&P 500 index fund providing even more income. So, why real estate? Real estate is romanticized as an investment for no reason other than it is tangible. A real product is great, but it doesn't mean you bought it for a fair price. It also makes no difference on whether or not you'll earn an appropriate return.

If it sounds like I don't like real estate, that's not true. Real estate makes a lot of sense for a particular class of investor, but I don't recommend it for everyday people with a little bit of cash burning a hole in their pocket. For my own portfolio, I appreciate real estate as a means of diversification or a passion project.

If you've decided you want to buy or invest in real estate, why do you like that? If it's about the returns, are you fully investing in your 401K and achieving the maximum match from your employer (essentially free money)? Does landlording fit into your schedule? Have you factored upkeep and maintenance into your estimated return on investment? Does real estate provide better returns than other assets? Is it the most passive of potentially passive investments? Are you naturally interested in real estate? If this sounds like a lot of work, that's because it is, and these questions are not even close to what professional analysts are required to answer to make intelligent investments. Banks and investment funds pay analysts billions annually to find suitable investments. Why would they pay those salaries if any jabroni on the street could easily do it?

Back to the earlier example, ask *why* about attracting women or attracting a type of woman. Ask why the $100,000 per year income goal will achieve better security. Perhaps spending less and tempering your expectations will provide more security, whereas a higher income may just prompt more desires, more spending, and less saving.

$100,000+ is a big jump from the current $40,000 salary. Beyond re-skilling, you're potentially looking at a complete personal overhaul requirement. Are you ready to do that? From personal experience, I can tell you it's very possible, but it is tough and takes years to achieve. Don't be discouraged; acknowledge it won't happen tomorrow or even next year. If you want it, you're in for a long ride.

Con artists try to sell you instant success and a 4-hour workweek, or a *bro* tells you he makes six figures, never did his

Ch. 3 Value

homework, and doesn't work hard at all. If true, these people won the lottery of life. Dig into your values framework if this is what you desire. Most likely, these people are playing your naivete and greed for their advantage, and the only lesson you'll learn is that you cannot replicate their *success*. Beware of anyone telling you it is easy.

Can you be happy with less money and lower expectations?

Lower expectations have a negative connotation, but it doesn't need to be bad. My wife and I decided she will not continue to a fellowship after medical residency because the extra income is not worth the effort. We value time for our family, and our incomes will be good enough without it. We have planned and budgeted for what we want. She will have competency and already earn sufficiently without additional training – extra training provides nothing of value to us. *More* is not valuable. Perhaps she will return later in her career if she desires.

I have another 30-year-old friend who is also a resident physician. She grew up in North Dakota in a working-class family. She aims to continue training after residency in a specialty that could make $1 million per year. That is her goal – to make a million dollars per year. And it is very possible. This is replicable success, but she is a medical doctor, the process is grueling, it requires an above-average level of intelligence, and there are very few people willing to put in the required effort to achieve this.

Exhaustion and burnout already ruin many of her nights and weekends, even when she is not working. She lives in a one-bedroom apartment with her cats and has no time to meet a partner. She currently earns enough money to go on vacations (residents make ~$65K per year), which is the most she has ever made. It's probably favorable to what her parents made. She could leave residency making between $200K-$400K per year without prolonging training and with a relatively decent work-life balance. There is almost nothing you can't do as a single person making that kind of money.

Continuing her path, she will never have a work-life balance – the specialty requires being on-call nights and weekends and has a high burnout rate (unsurprisingly). She is barely making it through residency due to exhaustion, but that potential salary keeps her going. Beyond the stress and student debt, she has/will sacrifice roughly 14 years of her life to achieve this goal – eight years of life for college, four for residency, and two years for a fellowship.

If this is what an intelligent medical doctor must go through to make a million dollars a year, why would you obtain it with less effort?

Moreover, if your goal is money, how do you know you need a million-dollar salary to buy what you want if you have yet to define what that is? If you've never made a $100K salary, why would you need 10x that? Not that you *need* something to want it, but very few purchases require that income level. What do you want? Is *more* a real answer?

Since separating from the military, I have earned in every interval from $20,000 per year to $100,000-plus. In the $20Ks, I begged my parents and friends to let me stay with them because I could not afford rent elsewhere. In the $30Ks, I could afford rent, insurance, and a little bit of going out. The $50Ks is where I noticed a significant improvement in quality of living. The lesser intervals required extensive prioritizing and budgeting (and panicking when I ran out of money), but the $50Ks allowed for more discretionary income, vacations,

Ch. 3 Value

and savings. I saved hardly anything up to that point.

Now that I'm well into the six figures, I cannot imagine what making more money would mean – as I said, my wife and I decided our prospective income (well below $1 million) will be good enough. Even the first year I made $75,000, I thought I was ballin' hard out of control – I had a great apartment downtown, went out for drinks any time I wanted, had no debt, was saving for retirement, and went on Caribbean vacations. Now that I earn more, I spend more on my house and my daughter, but the extra earnings are essentially just savings. Saving for what? I own a great home, I can refinish my drywall and lay tile myself and don't mind doing it if I have the time, and my wife has limited time for vacations as a resident.

This is not a tirade against the million-dollar goal. It's a valid goal if you know what you'll do when you achieve it. When I spoke to my friend about it, it didn't appear she understood the goal beyond "It's a million dollars!" Sounds great…

What does more money provide that less money cannot, and why are you willing to give up your life for it?

Pro-tip: A man once told me, "In the question of money or women, always choose money. Money can buy women, but women cannot buy you money. Unless they're hookers…"

Chapter Exercise: Values

Under the five categories below, list your top two values related to each. Be as descriptive or general as you'd like.

Family
(e.g., Traditions, holidays, helping your elderly parent or grandparents, having a large family of your own)

1.

2.

Social
(e.g., Best Friend, things you do with friends, picking up "chicks")

1.

2.

Hobbies
(e.g., Skateboarding, skiing, puzzles, video games)

1.

2.

Work
(e.g., Learning, skills development, work environment, roles)

1.

2.

Macro
(e.g., Anything that extends beyond yourself/family/friends – Social justice, politics, the economy)

1.

2.

Chapter 4:

Everything is a Tradeoff

In the prior chapter, we discussed my friend who is willing to do what it takes to make $1 million per year. She has invested years of her life, taken on a massive debt burden to support that goal, and sacrificed relationships.

It's not just what you are willing to do, but what are you willing to *not* do to meet your goal?

My other successful friend and mentor gave up his high school and college weekends and sex (although he never had any to begin with...). To party hard, my rowdy friend gave up any sense of wrong-doing, self-control, and friends.

In finance, we talk about *opportunity cost*: the analysis of a decision must include the cost of not selecting the alternative. The same is true for your life. Hidden in every choice is a decision not to choose something else. Regret is the feeling that we could have done better for what we gave up.

According to a study by economists at ZipRecruiter, 72% of Liberal Arts graduates regret their major. The other 28% just hadn't realized their mistake at the time of the survey… is what I imagine. The common trait for the most regretted degrees is that they do not provide tangible skills. Liberal Arts programs often provide grand theories that are hard to relate to action at the personal level. These theories are what I call the *macro* perspective, with the *micro* perspective relating to individual efforts and skills. The tradeoffs in education are skills vs. no skills, quantitative vs. qualitative, and the micro vs. the macro. We all must do something in the *micro* because nothing gets done without individuals taking action. Someone else will do it in the *macro* because statistics show certain things generally happen. A quality undergraduate degree provides a balance. In contrast, a trades program is all micro – you learn the correct actions a tradesman, as an individual, needs to take (i.e., a deep focus on tangible skills).

To illustrate the macro vs. the micro, consider a home remodeling project. Demo your bathroom, leave it, and return in six months. Did the statistic that 90% of home DIY projects are a success help complete the work? Of course not. This is a ridiculous example with a fake statistic; however, this is exactly how most people view other aspects of their lives, especially when selecting a college major.

In terms of *opportunity cost*, if you invest four years of your life as a gender studies major and graduate with $50,000 in debt, a $15 per-hour job, and a lack of marketable skills, you must also consider what you gave up – a more useful degree that teaches skills and the ability find opportunities for practical application of what you learned. The critical question is: What is it doing for you that you couldn't have done without it? Perhaps obtaining an engineering degree could provide

Ch. 4 Everything is a Tradeoff

the same ability to understand the world, but the increased earnings could help you create even more change. Engineering may teach you to balance the macro perspective with the micro and learn that individual actions matter quite a bit. Your life may change if you start producing a tangible product or learn to invest appropriately. Your increased salary may even help close the *wage gap*.

It's not just about what you obtained or gave up with a gender studies degree; it's what did you receive that you couldn't have gotten with another degree? The next question is: how meaningful is the difference? Many people talk about differences in programs without consideration of *materiality*. Once again, we must consider materiality in all that we do.

Tradeoffs are a primary consideration of investing. Financial advisors work with clients to understand their values, goals, timeframe, risk tolerance, and liquidity. The reason is to understand what options are available to that investor and which are not. My friend who wants $1 million in real estate has the risk tolerance (through naivete and ignorance) but lacks the capacity (the million dollars to invest). A person with poor credit, unstable income, and a lack of awareness of market fundamentals should not invest in real estate, no matter how high their risk tolerance is. On the other hand, a person with $1 million in cash, living in retirement, and with a low risk tolerance may reasonably consider real estate.

Risk and reward are the primary tradeoffs (low-risk, low reward, or high risk, high reward). Do you want low risk, high reward? Sorry, it does not exist. This is a fact.

Any imbalance between risk and reward in the public markets is balanced out by sophisticated traders and arbitrageurs who are paid millions of dollars annually to exploit inequalities and bring them back to balance. Unless that's you... well, it's not you, so there is no need to delve further. It's also not me.

Suppose you're 65 and invest 100% of your $1 million retirement account into OnlyFans. You may make massive gains (YOLO!) or lose so much more. You can lose your investment but also miss out on huge gains at Tesla, Apple, or an index fund. You may also be taking excessive risk (risk/reward imbalance), which reduces your *expected return* below that of investment alternatives. There is no such thing as low risk, high reward, but there are many opportunities for high risk, low reward – i.e., gambling and much of the stock trading done by retail investors. Also, making this investment means you cannot invest elsewhere. If you invest $1 million in a cryptocurrency and the value goes to $0, you lose a million dollars plus would-be gains on your next best alternative – if the S&P 500 index rises 30% in the same period, your loss is then $1.3 million because you gave up those potential gains over the period as well by choosing a poor investment. Or, in the Minneapolis condo scenario from the earlier chapter, the total loss to the current seller is almost 50% because they lost roughly 10% on a cost basis plus 40% from investing in a poorly performing market vs. the average market over the period. That's the opportunity cost.

Opposite of YOLO! another friend has been investing heavily in government debt since 2022. While U.S. Treasuries started paying the best returns we've seen in decades, I encouraged him to consider the constraints of the strategy and what he won't be invested in. He could face trouble selling his 3.5% bonds before maturity if rates rise further. This is not to discourage but to acknowledge the opportunity cost and risks involved with the strategy. Yes, even low-risk strategies have

Ch. 4 Everything is a Tradeoff

tradeoffs. He is unconcerned because he is solely looking for stability and a modest long-term return (U.S. government debt is considered *risk-free*, but only if you hold it to maturity). Fair enough, he knows why he's making his decision and is prepared for the long run – holding periods are a significant consideration for most investments. If you remember the bank failures of early 2023 (Silicon Valley Bank et al.), they essentially failed due to the risks I warned him about (which I did several months before the bank failures). Very surprisingly, he can withstand greater shocks to the U.S. Treasuries market than SVB through his longer holding period. But making this investment still means he is constraining his future actions.

After the trough of the Great Recession, the Dow Jones Industrial Average index has increased more than 500% since. Many homes that sold for $50K-$100K after 2008/09 are now worth 500%+ as much. Government debt will never produce that kind of return. Your actions do not just provide opportunity, but also constraints, and tying up your funds in other investments is a constraint. **What you do today will impact what you cannot do tomorrow.**

Obviously, risks are rising, and black swan events are becoming more of the norm since 2020. Historical gains are not certain to repeat themselves; however, good opportunities will emerge again.

Leading into 2022, we all heard about what a great investment real estate was. On the macro, it certainly was given the broad increases across markets. But was it an excellent investment everywhere? No, just as we showed earlier about the Minneapolis market. Let's explore the micro further.

I rented a condo in Downtown Minneapolis from 2017 to

2020. I paid $1,200 per month for a 1 bed/1 bath and was obtaining a hell of a deal because it was an older building with a lot of rules. New luxury one-bedroom apartments in the area rented for about $1,700 per month. My landlord was considering selling the condo for around $175,000. PITI (Principal, Interest, Property Taxes, and Insurance) plus the HOA fee would have increased my payment to over $1,500 per month (and I have an outstanding credit score with VA loan eligibility, providing the lowest potential cost with a similar down payment – meaning most others will pay more).

Details:

Asking price: **$175,000**

Down Payment: **5%**

PITI + HOA Fee: **$1,500**

Current asking monthly rent: **$1,200**

Increased monthly cost: **$300** = $1,500 - $1,200

Percentage Increase: **25%** = $300 / $1,200

Comparable 1 bed/bath unit sale prices: **$155,000**

We discussed the ludicrous increase and the lack of support at such a price. Forget the comparables valuations and the downpayment. Why pay $300 or 25% more per month just to own? It would take years for rents to catch up, which they may never do under normal circumstances. This landlord only increased my rent by $25 per month at my lease renewal. Other rents on the lower end of the market were rapidly rising, while this apartment, as well as new apartments' rents, were increasing very slowly. Differences in growth rates are essential

Ch. 4 Everything is a Tradeoff

because new apartments are the cap for prices, and no non-luxury older apartment will rent for more than the top-of-the-line newer unit in the same area. With that, how high could my rent go?

I estimated maybe $1,500 over several years, the equivalent of my prospective mortgage payment on the same property. I offered him $135K for the 1 bed/1 bath, which would have put me at roughly $1,350 per month. This would increase my costs for a few years, but hopefully, I make a return by the time I rent it to someone else. He declined. [5]

At the time of this writing, nicer units are selling for less than $135K, and nicer and larger 2 bed/2 baths are going for the same price the owner wanted for the 1 bed/1 bath ($175K) or less. There are a dozen units for sale in the complex, and many have been on the market for over a year – they're not selling even at discounted prices. Comparable units are listed for rent at roughly the same amount I paid more than four years ago.

Was I right? I honestly don't know, regardless of where prices are today. A *paper loss* on a condo won't ruin my life over the long term. Also, prices could have skyrocketed due to other macro factors, and I could have had a big *W*. But I'm glad I didn't buy regardless.

I ended up moving a year later. Buying that unit certainly would have made my current house unaffordable. I love my home. It gives me purpose, a hobby, and a beautiful place for my family. I have a space and payment I will be comfortable

---

[5] This differs from the standard way of analyzing a real estate investment because differences in cash outflows for renting vs. buying are a direct constraint for non-investor buyers. My payment goes up in the real world.

with for the long term – I'm not worried about short-term fluctuations in property values because my holding period is likely decades long. But if I bought that condo (even at a bargain), I would not have one of the things I value most. It's not just the money at stake.

Anything you choose is a choice not to do something else. If I bought that property, even at a reasonable price, I could not buy a property I love later. When you play video games until 4 am, you choose not to get a good night's sleep and be productive elsewhere. None of the video game players I know say their goal is to be good at *Call of Duty* or *Civilization*; despite spending so much time doing such they must be trying to go pro. If you want to be a professional video gamer, see my comments on buying lottery tickets above and my virgin friend...

This is not to say you're lazy or not on track to meet your goals if you spend time playing video games. We all need a break from life and enjoy leisure time in various ways. My wife is a U.S. Naval Academy graduate and nuclear engineering officer turned medical doctor. Before having our daughter, she would go to work, come home after, watch hours of TV per night, go to bed, and repeat that until I planned something or forced her to do things differently. She had no energy for anything else. I don't judge her. She is on track to meet her goals and is doing exactly what she is meant to do – to learn medicine and make it through training. This state is only temporary because she is progressing along the effort axis in our "Progression" graph accordingly, and work will become easier once she leaves training, providing capacity for other activities.

I cannot say you need to do more – you know you're doing something wrong if you're not meeting your goals.

Ch. 4 Everything is a Tradeoff

Also, consider only your expectations may need to be corrected...

If you spend your time playing video games, are overweight, and live in your parent's basement at 30 years old but are upset you can't find a *perfect 10 woman*, it won't happen. I hope I'm not the first to say this, but the tradeoff for that lifestyle is not meeting hot chicks. You have a values/reality mismatch and should work to align yourself better. Or, go buy a lottery ticket if you're so lucky.

I moved up about as quickly as possible in the Air Force but left the military thinking I was constrained because ranks required a certain time in service, and the private sector has no requirement. I romanticized being a business owner and over-prioritized making money over everything else. I had a college degree, was broke, and hated my job. I never thought I was making enough money and believed I could go further if I ran my own company.

My dad was a long-time landscaping sole proprietor; single-person company. Very working class. He worked from job to job and had no employees. He wanted to do something more significant, and so did I, so we started a C-Corporation and went off selling jobs. We struck gold on a large contract with a local HOA community through my dad's connections. Our company had nine employees at its peak. I worked a separate full-time job plus roughly full-time with the company, and my dad managed operations full-time. He hated managing employees, but he was making better money than before. I mostly liked running the business side of things and filling in where needed, but I hated working so much.

I had a very contentious relationship with my now ex-wife, given my workload and her demanding expectations – money, dishes, laundry, to worship her, and do everything else at the same time I worked what was essentially two full-time jobs. I prioritized making money and working over her or what she valued. When I proposed leaving my full-time job to support the business with all my attention, we could not come to an agreement – she also valued the security of my regular employment. I valued money in the moment. She wanted "X," and I wanted to give "Y" – we were incompatible. This goes both ways as she refused to give up anything for me, thus conflict.

I gave up everything in order to earn more money than I ever made (which was not significant enough at $70K per year). My marriage didn't last, and I lost my house in the settlement. The company also didn't last more than a few years because my dad and I had different risk tolerances and growth plans (i.e., values), and we were generally unhappy with how things were going. There are limits to the value of money alone, and the dissatisfaction we felt from running the company was unsustainable. The money was not enough. He continued running the company with no employees (just the way he liked it) for several years while I moved into finance.

This experience taught me money can provide opportunities for a good life, but working for money can destroy one. This is a common tradeoff, and something greater than economics must matter. We'll continue to explore this concern.

We tend to attribute others' success to what they're doing. The next time you feel the temptation, try thinking about what they're not doing. This is just as important.

Rob McElhenny, or "Mac," of *It's Always Sunny in Philadelphia* got extremely ripped in the show's later seasons. When *Men's Health* asked how he accomplished this, McElhenny modestly stated, "I'm gonna break it down for

Ch. 4 Everything is a Tradeoff

you, because it's actually quite simple, and anybody can do this. Anybody on the planet can do this. First thing's first: if you have job—like a 9-5 job—quit that. Do you like food? Forget about that. Because you're never going to enjoy anything you eat. Alcohol? Sorry. That's out. So what you need to do—you have a chef, right? Like a personal chef?— make sure the chef makes you a lot of chicken breast. And make sure you keep your caloric intake at a certain level. And as you go to your physician 2-3 times a week—just to monitor all your testosterone levels—because testosterone is important to building muscle. You're good friends with the trainer from Magic Mike? Arin Babaian. So you want to give Arin a call. And you want to make sure he's at your house and takes you to the gym at least twice a day, because you're gonna want to do your muscle-building in the morning and then your cardio in the afternoon. Now, do you have a family? Like a significant other or kids? Yeah, forget about them. You're not going to have time to deal with them."

I love that guy.

To summarize: What do you want? What are you willing to do? What are you ready to give up? Are you sure?

Pro-tip: Cut out everything you like, quit your job, hire the *Magic Mike* personal trainer and a personal chef, visit your doctor multiple times per week, and never see your family – it's that simple.

Chapter Exercise: Prioritizing Values

Copy your values from Chapter 3's exercise. Prioritize by ranking them 1 to 10 (1 being the highest priority). Cross out values ranked 6-10 assuming you have limited time and energy only for the first five.

<u>Family</u>
1.   Top 5? (Yes / No) Rank: _____
2.   Top 5? (Yes / No) Rank: _____

<u>Social</u>
1.   Top 5? (Yes / No) Rank: _____
2.   Top 5? (Yes / No) Rank: _____

<u>Hobbies</u>
1.   Top 5? (Yes / No) Rank: _____
2.   Top 5? (Yes / No) Rank: _____

<u>Work</u>
1.   Top 5? (Yes / No) Rank: _____
2.   Top 5? (Yes / No) Rank: _____

<u>Macro</u>
1.   Top 5? (Yes / No) Rank: _____
2.   Top 5? (Yes / No) Rank: _____

Which values do you not have time, money, or energy for?

_____

What are you receiving in return for the sacrifice?

_____

Chapter 5:

Do something, but don't do *anything*.

Be less like a shotgun and more like a sniper rifle.

Generals are the military's top brass, while younger officers specialize in a particular field (pilot, surface warfare, special forces, intelligence). Are you at the level of General? No, so pick something to specialize in. The more tangible, the better.

A shotgun approach to life can make you well-rounded, as diversity of experience tends to provide, but it will take very long to build momentum. It is more probable that you will become discouraged before accomplishing anything meaningful. Your lack of decision-making or having a specialization will prompt you to jump from opportunity to opportunity – moving but never getting to where you want to be. Many of us are stuck here for years. Listen up if you're not much better off today than a couple years ago.

Studies suggest that more options lead to worse decisions. Today, there's a fancy word for that: *decision fatigue*. Making a decision and sticking to it can be a freeing experience, as counterintuitive as it seems.

I could not pick anything in my twenties. I left the military and had no idea of what I truly wanted or how to get what I thought I wanted (money). I had a conditional offer of employment with the U.S. Secret Service, pending a background investigation. The process was long. Several months long just to receive the conditional offer. Then came the background paperwork. It was also extensive. I completed it and sent it in. During this time, my successful buddy (who built IT servers) approached me to start an IT consulting company. I thought, "Sure, why not?" I was sales/business; he was the specialist. We had big dreams. We spent time on our website, our message, who we're targeting, and all the "right" steps to set up a successful business. Did I know anything about IT consulting? No, but I was *smart*.

After submitting my background paperwork for the Secret Service, it was months before I heard back – they didn't receive the package, and I needed to re-fill it out and send it in again. This was devastating news. It took me an entire weekend to complete the paperwork the first time, and it was already such a long process. But my friend and I would become millionaires, so who cares? I never re-sent the paperwork.

We didn't become millionaires, either. I was unwilling to be the salesman required to kickstart the business. I thought we could make up for my lack of ability by spending money and time on other marketing. After about a year of struggling to make calls and not accomplishing much, we hung this idea up.

Ch. 5 Do Something, But Don't Do *Anything*

Looking back, it wasn't just my expectations that were distorted. I was going to school, working, trying to start a business, and applying for the Secret Service (which is a surprisingly effortful task). Of course, none of it worked out. Too many options, no decisions. If one option didn't work out, oh well, I'll just do something else. Years later, I did the same thing with the landscaping company – it didn't work out. Stupid. I was open to anything because of my lack of success. But this was also a chicken and egg situation – was I unsuccessful because I was doing the wrong things, or was I spread thin and making poor choices with too many options? I don't know.

Graduating with a finance degree was a favorable life-changing event because of the skills it taught me. Still, it should be noted that deciding on finance was a definitive moment – I chose finance over all other options after careful consideration. When I went back for finance, I quit my job, left the landscaping company, started an accounting/finance internship, and put my energy into working toward the one goal – to learn finance and obtain a job in banking. This is the beginning of things working out for me.

Do something, but don't do *anything*.

Or, learn to say no.

Many successful people say you should do what you love. There is good reason for this – money alone is never enough, trends change, and it usually does not pay to jump from one opportunity to the next. Your time may come if you just stick to what you are doing long enough. This is the only "luck" that is semi-replicable. I mentioned earlier that time destroys the fragile, but the volatility provided by time also creates opportunities for the well-positioned.

Certain fields consistently provide solid incomes, for example, those with a math or science focus – engineers, accountants, and medical doctors. These are very low-risk career choices (low variability in pay and less uncertainty in the job market). It has been said that more physics PhDs work in finance than in physics. Wall Street wants them because of their math abilities, and they make a hell of a lot of money. Many well-paid industries and roles desire math skills because they're transferable, valuable, and rare. Math skills are always in demand and the roles pay well. But not everyone has the capacity for those jobs, and there's nothing wrong with that.

Alternatively, real estate is very cyclical and doesn't take much sophistication to enter the industry – a modest level of cash for a down payment, a willingness to take on burdensome debt, and a rosy optimism about what awaits you as a landlord. The ease of entry, use of leverage, and naïveté explain the booms and busts that are outside of any individual's control. If you were a real estate agent or mortgage officer in 1999 and had a decent network, you probably experienced tremendous income growth through the early 2000s. Salespeople had to put the effort in to make deals, but the industry boomed because of external factors – real estate is very much driven by the macro.

Salesmen with no mortgage experience followed the trends, broke into the industry, earned very well during the boom, and went bust or pivoted to something new afterward. Some have yet to make that kind of money ever again. Suppose you were in the industry early on and set aside enough savings during the boom to get through the bust. In that case, you may have survived the financial crisis and had another hell of a run in the late 2010s and early 2020s.

Ch. 5 Do Something, But Don't Do *Anything*

Averaging your earnings out over the years, you did reasonably well – but the peaks do not represent the average, and the hard times are difficult to survive. Married couples went all-in on synergies, with the husband being the mortgage banker and the wife as a real estate agent or vice-versa and lost everything.

Many staked everything on real estate during the COVID era as there was no end to the housing boom in sight. Unfortunately, 2022 brought higher rates and abysmal home sales. Mortgage departments announced mass layoffs, and it's all over again. Some will survive. The most sophisticated bankers, investors, and agents may make it through. They have enough experience to know it never lasts forever and presumably set aside a large nest egg to make it through the trough or retire altogether; however, it is extremely difficult for individual effort to make up for a weak macro environment. Unless you've developed your business correctly.

During the 2000s real estate boom, my friend's brother worked a construction job and owned and rented out several homes. He bragged about making a few hundred thousand dollars a year and owning millions of dollars in assets. Except he didn't. Yes, he owned several homes, and yes, he may have *grossed* a few hundred thousand dollars a year from rents, but *net* cash flows weren't that large, and those weren't *net* assets. Remember the earlier examples about debt service on the mortgage debt. He had loans on everything and massive mortgage payments. Who cares how much the homes are appraised for if your tenants stop paying rent and you cannot make the payments you owe nor find a buyer for that price? This is what happened to him. His tenants were his only source of cash flow because his construction job projects ceased

Ch. 5 Do Something, But Don't Do *Anything*

in this period, so he struggled along with his tenants, who also mostly worked construction-related jobs. He leveraged himself to the tits against the real estate industry: his career was real estate-related, his investments were related, and all sources of tenant cash flow indirectly came from the same types of real estate. This guy never heard of diversification. You can guess what happened.

Yes, he lost everything.

Living on top of the world for about two years. Nothing to show for it today. He couldn't be on the mortgage when his wife bought a house several years after the crash. My friend got stuck with a home 50 miles from his office that his investor brother talked him into buying. His brother owned part of the home but couldn't make his proportional contribution to the mortgage after losing everything. My friend had a solid job but was forced to move, drive over an hour to and from work every day, couldn't sell the house except at a massive loss, and wasn't able to take advantage of tremendous opportunities in the market later because he bought this house at the peak. Several years and thousands of dollars' worth of upgrades later, he broke even on the sale and said good riddance.

Before my friend sold, he had some hail damage on his siding, and his investor brother wanted the contract to fix it. His brother cried to his mom – literally – when his offer to repair the siding was turned down (he was also kind of a crook). My friend receives a call from his crying mother because he is not supporting the family in trying times. She stresses how badly his brother needs the work and guilts my friend into throwing his brother a bone. His brother was ruined by the crash, both financially and emotionally. He's never recovered.

Ch. 5 Do Something, But Don't Do *Anything*

You're probably wondering, "If nobody is making money, then where does it all go?" which is a valid question. Someone does make money – brokers mostly, but it's temporary. Also, the guy who owned for 5, 10, or 20 years has never experienced a market so out-of-control and decided to cash out. They were *positioned* for success. The other winners are very sophisticated and bought into the market early enough in the craze and monitored it carefully, knowing it could not last forever. Lastly, a few others get really lucky and sell at the right time – which is not replicable.

The point is not to scare you into never taking a risk. Risk-taking is a necessary endeavor. For all anyone knows, the real estate market could have boomed for another few years in both the 2000s and 2020s. But most people lost everything in the 2000s because they took **excessive risk** – it helped them build a small empire in just a few years, but they lost it more quickly than it came. We'll see what the 2020s have in store.

Excessive risk in this situation can be identified by (a) leveraging up rapidly, (b) limited diversification, (c) following an unsustainable trend, and (d) relying on a sucker to cash them out.

You are leveraging up rapidly if you're buying your next property with loans based on cash flow from a property you've only owned for a short period.

Most people think of diversification as a portfolio of stocks, bonds, real estate, and commodities. Still, you can get so much more granular. Diversification is a range, not an absolute.

You can diversify even if investing solely in residential real estate through geography, neighborhood, demographics, and price range. If you buy five houses on the same street, your tenants are probably of similar demographics and socioeconomic class. They may even work in related industries. If this neighborhood booms, you may win big, but you have no diversification if it is adversely impacted – excessive risk (let's say the local manufacturing plant shutters and they all lose their jobs). Demographic diversification relates to my friend's brother – he rented solely to construction workers in the metropolitan outskirts. When construction jobs stopped coming, none of them could pay their rent – excessive risk.

You can mitigate this risk through geographic diversification (city vs. suburbs vs. rural) and price range. Yuppies (Young Urban Professionals) or DINKS (Dual- income, no kids) may want the million-dollar loft in the downtown city center vs. a $300K house in a suburb. It also depends on how you market your properties. You can also apply this granularity to diversification in a stock or other portfolio – imagine a pharmaceutical-specific ETF. Some pharma startups win big on a new drug, while many may bust or encounter FDA rejection. Even if pharmaceuticals is the right industry to invest in, do you want all of your eggs in one basket by betting it all on one company or drug?

REIT investments can provide the benefit of diversification of a real estate portfolio along with professional management, and they are actually *passive*. Some experienced massive gains in the COVID era; however, very few REITs *go to the moon*. Nobody becomes rich by investing a few dollars in a REIT stock. Why? REITs are typically diversified, and one-off lottery-type gains are stripped by declines elsewhere, as you may expect with diversification. Diversified, you will hardly do better than a REIT composed of similar assets (such as residential real estate). The massive gains you desire are a product of excessive, lottery-type risk. Don't be fooled – there is a gross mismatch between the

Ch. 5 Do Something, But Don't Do *Anything* 77

risk and reward here, and you're much more likely to lose than to win big. That doesn't mean you won't win, but go buy a lottery ticket if you're so lucky. We're focusing on the sustainable and replicable.

Many businesses use excessive risk as a competitive advantage, but it's unsustainable. By its nature, excessive risk has an expected value of less than $0 over the long run. Simplified: You are just gambling. Sometimes you win, but you will lose if you play enough. Nassim Nicholas Taleb would call you *fragile*. How do you know if you're gambling vs. just taking average risk? You desire getting rich quickly. Successful businesses are built organically over the medium- to-long term unless the investor flows to the company are large *and* management is sophisticated.

As an investor, assets and investments provide comfort as a store of wealth and provide modest returns. But you must have wealth. If you're seeking wealth by investing, you're just gambling.

This is not automatically wrong, but the wise suggest only gambling with what you are willing to lose. You must also consider where you stand in the *investor food chain*.

The *investor food chain* is who eats who in investing. *Eating* in this context is realizing gains before others. The most sophisticated investors are at the top of the food chain – hedge funds, private equity, investment bankers, and politicians. Then, the well-informed bankers, economists, and industry-specific insiders. Next, bankers or financial advisors who are actually just salespeople with access to economic research they never bother to read (most bankers and advisors are just salespeople). Then, your buddy making tons of money on an investment. Lastly, you.

The guy who has been invested for the long term and cashes out is near the top of the food chain because he knows the local environment better than most. These guys exist in every boom industry – they are the well-positioned and whom you should strive to become if you want in on the gains.

If you're hearing about a *good deal* from your recently invested buddy, just remember, he's last unless he finds a sucker to offload his shit onto – this is why you are last. Narratives play a vital role in finding investors.

The home flipper of yesteryear turned into the short-term rental rockstar. 9 out of 10 of my Airbnb hosts have been bomb-shell blondes or super trendy dudes in their late 20s (according to their profile picture). It's very coincidental that everyone is really good-looking and young in this industry. Must be because it's so easy!

If buying a home, putting a little bit of cash into it, and renting it on Airbnb is an easy way to make money, then rich people will exploit those returns out of the market. Home prices rise disproportionately to rental rates, and the good deals are worked out of the system, which almost certainly occurred during the COVID-era boom.

Diversified wealth can afford to test a new idea, can you? Remember, you're buying a home with a decades-long payment but are only receiving nightly rates – how easily the macro environment could shift over the next 20 to 30 years (if not in the next three to five). Also, fund managers invested heavily in real estate. If outsized gains are to be made here, they will have their finger in it.

Governments printed so much cash from 2008 to 2022 that the most sophisticated firms paid top dollar to analysts who could find good deals in any market to make multiples on any

Ch. 5 Do Something, But Don't Do *Anything*

investment. I mentioned earlier that there are no good deals in the public markets, but government cash printing and private equity funds ensured there are no longer good deals in the private markets either. Funds bought up thousands, if not millions, of housing units starting in the early 2010s. Healthcare? They are buying up healthcare clinics, too. They have their fingers in everything, harvesting all the gains from the current operations and hoping some jabroni will copy their move and pay an even higher multiple. The investor food chain matters because these entities are watching much more closely than you are to recognize the peak, and they will sell out before you. When you finally realize it is time to sell, it may be too late with too few buyers.

If you already decided real estate was an industry catching your interest and owned several homes for many years, you could convert your current units to Airbnb's and probably make outstanding returns. If you bought a house in the COVID-era or later and expected to win big, you're almost certainly too late. And if you were anything other than lucky, you could put your skills to use at an investment fund and make much more money than you could on a few rental properties.

As stated earlier, you can increase your returns by spending time keeping up the property, but then you must convert your hours into a cost against the returns and consider what else you could have been doing – i.e., what is the opportunity cost of your labor? Also, from the perspective of opportunity cost, you don't need to lose money to make it a lousy investment – bad simply means worse than your alternatives. If you love doing this, then this is not a consideration. Hobbies do not require returns. But if this is an investment, you must consider and incorporate all costs into your analysis. Not including these costs and overestimating returns is why so many people rush into bad investments.

Jay Gajavelli built a $700 million real estate empire during the COVID era made up of thousands of housing units. Before starting his fund, he worked in IT and grew up lower- middle-class in India. He doesn't appear to have any prior professional real estate experience, but the concept of *passive income* changed Jay's life. He helped small investors break into real estate by offering to them a portion of his investments that he planned to buy, fix up, jack up the rents, then sell for massive profit – double your money in just a few years. Building his empire was so easy and riskless that Jay commented, "I never worry about the economy now" because people always need a home. Why isn't everyone doing this!?!

He is now highlighted in a recent Wall Street Journal article. According to the WSJ, "Few investors rode the pandemic-era housing boom as high… Fewer still have fallen as far." Yes. Gajavelli's business empire is crumbling because it was riddled with excessive risk, and 3,000 of his units were lost to foreclosure by early 2023. The future of his empire is uncertain, but this is already one of the largest residential real estate fund blowups since the housing bubble burst. Investors have lost millions of dollars. Lenders will also lose millions.

As his property managers raised monthly rents, cash flow suffered as more tenants became past due. An introductory economics course could help Gajavelli understand constraints to pricing – people will not automatically pay a higher price, despite *always needing a home*. This idea has been perpetuated to the masses in the post-COVID era, but think of the logic here. Why don't food prices jump to the moon, or clothing, or gasoline – these are all essentials. In fact, oil is a great example. Once it gets too high people adjust their behaviors, and

Ch. 5 Do Something, But Don't Do *Anything*

the price drops despite *always needing transportation*.[6]

Additionally, more than $115 billion was pumped into similar investing schemes since 2020, and the WSJ states many more of these managers are "racing to either raise funds or sell properties before tipping into foreclosure." I'm sure Gajavelli tried raising additional funds, so perhaps there's only one option left – sell. Oh wait, that's also what you usually do before foreclosure... Most likely, he overpaid for his properties and is now underwater on the related debt. Being underwater leads to foreclosure because units cannot be sold above their mortgaged amounts in a reasonable time frame. Both the owner and lender prefer a standard sale over a foreclosure or short sale due to costs associated with such, the reputational damage, and the risk of driving fear into the market.

Beyond the financial, people are impacted by these decisions. Real people lived in Gajavelli's properties that he neglected and subjected to squalor conditions when he wasn't making enough on his investments. Jumping into an investment where you haven't considered the reality and the actual costs of ownership end with cutting expenses for routine services, which impacts people's lives and is truly unethical. Gajavelli didn't understand what it takes because property management was new to him and obtaining funding was so easy. This is all

---

[6] I understand that inflation has impacted all these items and it feels like food prices have gone to the moon. But this is not because everyone *always needs food*. People have always needed food, just as they've always needed a home. Inflation is a post-COVID/money-printing/quantitative easing phenomenon, as were skyrocketing real estate values.

expected when money is cheap, and your fund manager is a social media *influencer*.

Per an August 2023 WSJ article, the $6.5 billion fund, Tides Equities, grew tremendously with a strategy similar to Jay Gajavelli. In 2021, they expected to raise rental rates by 44% over the next few years. However, the *tides turned* in 2023 when that strategy wasn't going as planned. Some properties are no longer collecting enough rents to offset debt payments (according to the company), and investors will need to invest more in failing properties or risk default. The list of excessive risk-takers in the real estate sector goes on and on, and these stories are becoming more common. I use so many examples of real estate because most unsophisticated investors believe it is *the* easy way to get rich. There are many easy ways to get rich. All of which have many easy ways to lose it all.

Positioning is essential, and why those with a long-term focus get lucky.

It's just not your typical investments or industries, either. I gifted my brother all of my old *Magic: The Gathering* and *Pokémon* playing cards in the early 2010s. I got into these games in the mid-to-late 1990s and started collecting Pokémon cards immediately following its U.S. release. I owned a foil Charizard Pokémon card and certainly had many more valuable cards. If you didn't play and have no idea what that is, first-edition Charizard cards have sold for tens of thousands of dollars. I had that, and I gave it away. I had no idea it would be worth anything. But now that card's time has come. The return would be over 20,000% if I just held on. My brother also gave away those cards (at least, that is what he told me). We held onto them for 20 years but gave them away just before the boom.

Ch. 5 Do Something, But Don't Do *Anything* 83

This is an example of poor positioning.

Alone, you cannot afford to act like a hedge fund, monitor every market, or have your fingers in everything. You'll be burned if you lollygag in to opportunities at the last minute. You may achieve outsized returns when the time comes if you stick to what you're doing long enough. Chasing *anything* leads to a lack of focus and can only bring you success for a short period. More likely, it never materializes at all because you don't specialize deeply enough and aren't positioned for the long term when opportunities arise. Furthermore, false narratives are perpetuated to offload dogshit onto less sophisticated investors. The longer you stick with something, the more sophisticated you will become.

Professional financial advisors can be of great value to help you develop an investment strategy and find appropriate investments with in your budget and risk tolerance. Many have no minimum asset requirements and are helpful as a sounding board, even if you have a solid idea of your goals and can invest independently. Talking through your strategy, no matter how simple, can help you formulate additional ideas, find new opportunities, or to surface risks you didn't realize you were taking. They can also keep you accountable to your goals. Beware of *influencer* advisors/ investors.

There have been calls in recent years to remove asset requirements for hedge fund and private equity investors. These funds have investor size requirements because they use very sophisticated methods susceptible to outsized losses. People who meet the thresholds are presumably willing and capable of taking the risk because they have other means or diversified investment. Those calling for removing requirements cite the outsized specific investments. Think of the great returns for private investors in Uber or Lyft, Facebook, and others after going public – early Uber investors turned $100,000 into $300 million; Facebook turned $500,000 into $1 billion, etc. What they don't mention is that early investors often lose 100% of their investment, and it's always **after** the great opportunities that sophisticated investors try to help *the little guy*. Perhaps they just need someone to pass the buck to.

GWG Holdings is/was an investment firm offering a chance for mom-and-pop investors to get in on private equity returns through its relationship with Beneficient. This relationship "kicked off what became one of the biggest financial blowups to strike retail investors in years" says the Wall Street Journal after GWG Holdings defaulted on $2 billion of debt and filed for bankruptcy. Twenty-eight thousand retail investors and retirees stand to lose over a billion dollars in savings. The company has few tangible assets to support a fruitful liquidation to repay investors. Beneficient recently separated from GWG, went public via a special- purpose acquisition company (you may have heard the term *SPAC*), and was "valued" at $3.5 billion. It raised only $8 million. At the time of this writing, the stock is down 85% from its opening public price, and both companies are under investigation by the Securities and Exchange Commission. Broker-dealers who referred investors are under investigation, and some have already gone bankrupt.

You're out of the game if you are undiversified and lose 100% of your total investment. It doesn't matter how well other investments do later. Average returns do not matter after losing everything. Neither do unicorn returns. One loss, and you're done. Many of Jay Gajavelli's and GWG's investors are

Ch. 5 Do Something, But Don't Do *Anything*

in this situation as they went all-in on the scheme that promoted unusually large returns.

These narrative promoters also don't mention the illiquidity of private investments – you cannot pull your funds at will. Liquidity matters. What if the required holding period is five years, but you need the money today? (Actually, don't worry because Beneficient allows you to trade your private equity investment for shares of Beneficient, a company that lost 85% of its value in less than 60 days from going public, is reporting massive losses, and is under investigation by the SEC – Awesome!) Despite my friend's brother owning several homes, he had no liquidity – cash on hand – and the market was equally illiquid – he couldn't sell the homes for what he owed in a reasonable time frame. Thus, foreclosure. He owned roughly $2 million worth of homes but had limited cash. If he had even a modest level of stable cash (approximately $100K), he might have been able to last long enough to rent out his homes again when the economy recovered, and he would be much better off today. But he followed the same get-rich-quick advice Jay Gajavelli and so many others have. He never held material liquidity because he pumped everything he had into the next property to multiply his assets – excessive risk – with nothing to cushion a setback.[7]

Within days of writing this section, Silicon Valley Bank's failure presented another example of illiquidity. The bank posted profits every year for several years, grew dramatically through the COVID era, and still folded when dynamics

---

[7] $100K is not a significant hold in my friend's situation because this guy was "making" a few hundred thousand dollars a year and owned millions of dollars of real estate. A few hundred thousand in cash should have been a given for someone with those means.

shifted. There's more to it, but a lack of liquidity was the primary cause of their failure. 16th largest bank in the U.S. prior to collapse and the second largest bank failure of all time. Also, somewhat coincidentally, the Gajavelli, Tides, and GWG stories all made national headlines *after* I wrote this section about the risks of the related strategies, and I added the examples later. Fragile, anyone? (We'll see many more examples in the years to come.)

Other banks are doing conceptually the same thing as the PE investors, but for minority communities and real estate – they are passing the buck. At the peak of home values in 2022 and after the central banks began raising rates, several of the largest lenders began offering no-cash down payment loans for minority communities. It is very well- known home values and rates are inversely correlated (home values decline when rates rise, and vice versa), but they want to promote homeownership to communities historically locked out of the market at its peak – why the initiatives now?

In the context of the *investor food chain*, these buyers are the least sophisticated of all potential buyers because neither they nor their families have experience owning assets (per the narrative for why they need such assistance). The banks and sellers are certainly more sophisticated.

The real estate bubble devastated minority community homeownership, with so many losing their homes after the crash, and this is well-known. Weak mortgage underwriting standards in the early 2000s improved minority ownership for only a few years before they declined **below** pre-2000 levels after the crash. Thousands lost homes and were worse off after the dust settled. Someone else got those funds; money doesn't just disappear. Why did it take nearly 15 years to

Ch. 5 Do Something, But Don't Do *Anything*

prompt this new initiative, and why did it occur as market dynamics weakened?

Is this malicious intent?

Market values tend to rise until the *last marginal investor* invests. The *last marginal investor* is the person who is either too skeptical or incapable of investing until now. Historically excluded groups – people of color in communities predominantly of people of color – would be the last marginal investors in the context of homeownership. Perhaps they would like to buy, but underwriting standards are too strict (required credit scores and income ratios), or they lack the funds necessary for a downpayment and closing costs (which the federal government has recently reduced to entice additional demand, er, I mean, "help communities of color"). Removing those barriers provides opportunities for that group to now participate. This is conceptually similar to why home values boomed during the early 2000s as underwriting standards were eliminated – the pool of buyers increased dramatically (i.e., supply and demand).

Real estate values can continue to rise or maintain their values if the number of buyers is sufficient. By increasing the number of applicants/buyers through these programs, the banks help stabilize their current loans' collateral values and increase the likelihood of being repaid on old mortgages, even if the new mortgages are riskier. Suppose the number of prospective buyers declines (relative to supply). In that case, homes will lose value – which happened in many areas from 2022 to 2023 – and foreclosures are likely to follow if the trends continue and the economy weakens. It's probably a futile attempt by the banks and government.

Am I predicting a real estate collapse? Not exactly, but I would be hesitant to buy at peak prices with rising rates (correlated with declining values in the mid-to-long term), and as fewer people are willing and able to take the buck I may need to pass (declining demand and reduced liquidity in the market). This is an acknowledgment of risk, not advice to delay buying a home. Suppose you buy at an affordable monthly payment and benefit from a $0 down payment and lower closing costs. In that case, the risk is significantly reduced – the initial investment is near zero, and the primary risk is then affording the payment over the long term. Paper losses don't ruin you until you need to sell.

As self-serving as these initiatives suggest about the banks and proponents of these plans, this doesn't need to be bad for these communities. Buyers have a good opportunity if they maintain a long-term focus. People on the margins often only obtain opportunities when the elites have depleted other options. Do not squander this opportunity with a short-term strategy filled with excessive risk-taking (e.g., buying at a high or adjustable rate hoping rates lower in the near term in order to afford the payment, purchasing multiple properties thinking you can still quickly flip them, or allowing FOMO to take hold and turning purchases into AirBnB-type rentals). Don't be the one without a chair as the music stops. And it will stop at some point. A longer holding period on an affordable payment dramatically reduces these risks.

Banks require a commercial loan to have two sources of repayment. The first is cash flow from operations – the company sells a product and generates a profit. The second is usually some collateral – property or equipment – but banks have been relying on *refinancing* as a secondary source (i.e., another lender pays the first lender off) to justify lending to leveraged and asset-light companies. Secondary sources are relied upon if the business can no longer repay the loan with

Ch. 5 Do Something, But Don't Do *Anything*

cash. I never understood refinancing as a source of repayment as it is only relied upon if the borrower cannot repay the loan by operating. Very few lenders are willing to lend to a borrower who is demonstrably unable to repay a debt, especially since most defaults occur in weakened economies when lending standards tend to be the tightest.

Banks are currently moving away from refinancing as an acceptable source. See, the problem with relying on refinancing as a source of repayment is conceptually similar to the short-term investor hoping to pass the buck. Refinancing requires you to find another bank willing to take on more risk – in other words, to find *the greater fool*. This was allowed when the economic outlook was bright, the government was printing cash, and banks were flush and competing heavily. Times have changed, and banks have tightened their belts. I presume banking regulators no longer believe there are enough fools to take out the potentially bad loans. Regulators are expecting losses from loans in this trillion-dollar market to be much greater than originally anticipated. Only time will tell how this turns out.

Everyone wants to pass the buck. People take excessive risk today if they believe someone else will take on more risk later. This explains why companies like Theranos and FTX could scam sophisticated investors – the investors knew the scam but thought they could sell out early enough. They are also not investing their own money – many are investing client money. Sometimes they win, sometimes they lose, but these firms always collect fees no matter the losses.

Bernie Madoff reported that his investors knew he was running a Ponzi scheme but still invested because they didn't believe they would be the last investors in the scheme.

In 2023, Billy McFarland secured funding for the revived Fyre Festival 2.0, despite spending years in prison following the fraudulent original Fyre Festival in 2017. Investors will give this guy another chance with millions of dollars, but well-paying jobs are hard to come by? The investors deserve to lose it all again.

In his spring 2023 guest appearance on the *Odd Lots* Bloomberg podcast, Nassim Nicholas Taleb spoke about how the Federal Reserve reducing rates to zero for fifteen years changed the finance culture from investing for future cash flows to investing in order to pass the buck later at a greater price. We have an entire elite tech industry class who became extremely rich due to easy-money policy, many without ever creating real value. These were essentially transfer payments from one investor to another, from investors to workers, or from investors to consumers (we'll discuss the façade of transfer payments in a later chapter). As good of a deal as that may be for a few, it's not value-creation. Value creation is necessary, and has little to do with price.

We are a pass-the-buck culture. Don't take the buck unless you understand the risks you are taking and are capable of taking them – otherwise, you'll accept *anything* and lose it all, like GWG, Fyre Festival, or Jay Gajavelli's investors.

Chapter Exercise: Excessive Risk

Detail a time when you jumped at an opportunity without thoroughly considering your other options or the full repercussions.

1.

Did it work out? (Y / N)

If so, could you or another person replicate the success?

(Y / N)

Chapter Exercise: Conversations

Remember your last few conversations with friends, family, or informal discussions with work colleagues. Write down three of the subjects in which you talked about and score them using a 1-10 range.1 being the lowest priority in your life and 10 being the highest priority based on your values identified in the Chapter 3 Exercise.

1.   Score _____
2.   Score _____
3.   Score _____

                                                    Total Score: _____

The higher the score, the more aligned your conversations are with your values. (Talk is cheap, so perhaps repeat the exercise with the last few activities you pursued).

Are you satisfied with the results? (Y / N)

Chapter 6:

Statistics Matter

Some say it's better to be lucky than good. If you're lucky, why not compound the potential success by being both?

Despite using the term *luck*, I don't believe in luck. What people call *luck* is really just *chance*. I don't mean to nitpick, but calling it luck implies there is nothing you can do about a situation – which is generally false. You can change your *chances* of something occurring (i.e., probability).

How do you increase your chances of finding a good job? Have in-demand skills in a growing field, apply for many opportunities, and call your network or companies directly. How do you increase the chances of selling a product? Find your target market and contact more of those people. Ever heard sales (or picking up women at a bar) is a numbers game? It's because the more you contact and get the word out, the more likely your product is to sell. This is illustrated in sales models that show how leads/contacts turn into meetings,

meetings turn into proposals, and proposals turn into sales. Need to reach a level of sales? Start with the top figure (leads) and hit that number; the rest generally follows.

Want to know what salary to ask for? Do some research and find appropriate statistics. Just because your buddy says he makes $150,000 per year as an entry-level salesman doesn't mean you will make the same (*attribution bias* is discussed later – people often mistake the reason for an occurrence, such as the success of your friend, and fail to find the true origin). Likewise, just because your parents tell you $15 per hour is a good wage, it does not mean you should only ask for that either. The government collects data on pretty much everything. Very informative is the U.S. Bureau of Labor Statistics to find regional salaries for job types. This is relatively granular, and job titles don't always represent the same work, so make sure your role's responsibilities match their descriptions.

The Robert Half Salary Guide is updated annually based on research within their target industries, and I have found it representative of reality. Find the appropriate resource if the above do not provide data on your industry or role. Avoid online posts by random people the best you can – are they real, fake, competitors, or recruiters posting to motivate you to act? What are the individual circumstances of the anonymous salary poster? Perhaps their father is a VP at the company or a vendor/customer (it's more common than you may think), and they received a great deal. Perhaps they are a giant turd, explaining their low salary or negative review. You don't know.

Broad averages that account for years of experience are best for reference if you are a random applicant with no strong connections to the company. You may still do better than average depending on the position, company, and/or labor market constraints, so be aware of the environment. The purpose here is to set your expectations appropriately, not to undersell yourself. If you have an *in*, use it.

Most banking analysts have a degree in finance or accounting – all you do for the first year or two is review borrower financial statements, so understanding finance is essential. A coworker of mine was a freshly graduated commercial banking analyst. I asked her: "Did you major in finance or accounting?"

Her: "No."

(It was an either/or question, so I was confused by the blunt "No" response.)

Me: "Did you take accounting electives or just have an excellent grasp of accounting and finance?"

Her: "No. I was a marketing major. I only took the intro accounting class and don't understand it well, honestly."

Me: "Oh... How did you get this job?"

Her: "I graduated, and my dad called the department head. He set it up."

If you're thinking about how awesome that would be, also consider how *awful* it would be to fill a role for which you are not qualified. I have a strong understanding of accounting and finance and struggled for years in the same position. I cannot imagine the self-doubt and ever-present uncertainty she is facing. She may feel it forever.

Except *she* won't. I do not feel sorry for the trust-fund- baby whose *Daddy* gifted her a well-paying job like it was a pony for Christmas. More likely than not, her incompetence will never

Ch. 6 Statistics Matter

show through because *Daddy* also bought her mentorship and a lack of real responsibility – she will never deal with problems. If she does, someone else will solve them (or management will rationalize all of her bad decisions away, and she will avoid consequences). This is the corporate class; they are treated like royalty with training wheels the entire way.

I mention the uncertainty of being unqualified for her role to help you conceptualize the struggle you may face if the luck you're waiting for pans out. You have your dream job you didn't work for, but *Daddy* isn't there to support you. The money may be great (for as long as it lasts), but you will experience the intense anxiety of uncertainty. Does *faking it 'til you make it* fit into your values?

Could you learn to do any job with some on-the-job training? Think again, as this perspective indicates a lack of experience in anything meaningful and minimizes hard-working people's contributions. Low-paying jobs are usually just running processes someone else has developed and require limited judgment – anyone with an IQ above 90 can learn simple processes, which is why those positions tend to pay like shit. Well-paying jobs are challenging, require skills and judgment, and take years to develop an appropriate perspective. A master plumber does not earn the title in less than several years, and a $200K-per-year analyst job requires extensive skill and perspective that no company will just sit there and teach you (excluding the *Daddy's* girl). Your buddy is in a position where he makes tons of money with no effort? Good for him; he won the lottery. You didn't. You want to win the lottery, go buy a ticket and wait your turn.

If you could snap your fingers and become CEO of your company with all the perks, pay, and responsibility, would you do it? How long could you last before everyone finds out you're a fraud? If you didn't work for it, you didn't earn it. You're not qualified if you don't have a comprehensive understanding of what drives your business and how it operates. And even if you do, you're probably still not qualified. Don't let that discourage you – very few people are CEOs. I'm not qualified to be CEO, *and* I failed at running my own small company – it's OK not to be CEO today, and you can find success elsewhere. We are working to develop the necessary skills so that perhaps it may happen someday if it's what you want.

A philosophical question of morality is raised in a situation determined solely by chance. Two parents leave their babies unattended in the bathtub, and one baby dies. Is one parent morally worse than the other? Do we accept that nothing terrible happened to the fortunate baby, and therefore, the parent did nothing wrong?

My life has been filled with "baby in the bathtub" type moments; yours is likely the same. These may not be situations of questionable morality, but they relate to you getting what you want. Are you getting by because you're making the right decisions or because chance hasn't turned a corner yet? Alternatively, is chance catching up with your excessive risk-taking or bad habits making life extra difficult?

Simply, have you ever examined your spending and found that the most minute discretionary items dominate your spending when aggregated – trips to the gas station for an energy drink, a pack of cigarettes, or a 6-pack of beer? Perhaps a daily coffee from Starbucks has taken a toll on your finances. Individually small, but these poor habits eat away at your financial health. Do you still blame your employer for screwing you on pay? Of course, that was a silly question…

Ch. 6 Statistics Matter

Spending is easy to identify when you use a debit/credit card but much harder if you pay with cash. The point is your habits and the things you do regularly impact the rest of your life and may be much more severe than minor spending items.

Have you ever met a guy who proclaims he has shit luck because he got fired from his job because his boss is an asshole, not because he cuts corners; his girlfriend dumped him because she's a bitch, not because he cheated on her; his car broke down because it's a piece of shit not because he half-asses maintenance; or the IRS wants the income taxes he never paid; and so on and on?

Sure, nepotism makes life easier for some (like *Daddy's* girl), and some people have disproportionately unfavorable chance events happen to them. I have repeated I am not lucky, but I am not unlucky either. I've had unfortunate events and medical conditions for which I could do nothing. My wife almost died giving birth to our daughter after complications arose late in pregnancy. Being overburdened with work and on a tight schedule, my wife ignored critical symptoms as they worsened to the point that required hospitalization, inducing labor, and lab work every 2 hours to ensure her condition didn't deteriorate. Fortunately, she recovered, and our baby is healthy. It could have been worse. Shit happens, and some things you do not control.

A good friend from banking lost his arms and legs to leukemia in his early adulthood. He was dealt a shit hand, and nobody would have blamed him for staying home, sulking in despair, and collecting disability. But he didn't. He finished college, came to work daily, and made many friends. We met for happy hours, talked about investments, and laughed a lot. He is a great inspiration. Your or my shit *luck* is nowhere nearly as bad as his. Sometimes, there's just nothing you can do, and you must move on with what you can. Many service members suffer injuries, disabilities, or worse. Serving is a dangerous activity. There is very little within your power to stop such events from happening short of living like a bubble boy. But so much of my life is my choice. Are you the protagonist in the film of your life, or are you an *extra*?

Upon this realization, I work to increase or decrease my chances of certain events in my power, and I don't take excessive risks blindly. This doesn't mean bad things can't happen by pure chance, as many wounded veterans and my friend with leukemia illustrate. Still, we must make an effort in the things we can control so that chance works favorably toward us when possible. We control what field we study, the time we spend on which tasks, the *excessive* risks we take, and how much effort we put into anything.

Pro-tip: If you have that girl's Daddy, expect a *good deal*. If not, follow the statistics.

Ch. 6 Statistics Matter

Chapter Exercise: Connections

Think of a position you want. List the people you know connected to that firm or the hiring manager. If you don't know anyone directly connected, list those with the closest connection in your network.

Company/position: _____

Connections:

1.

2.

3.

4.

5.

How can you better develop your network?

_____

Chapter 7:

To Be or Seem to Be, That is the Question.

Influencers. Insta-models. SBF.

The number one desired career path for American Gen Z'rs is *influencer*. The more appropriate description of this career path is *lottery winner* or perhaps *welfare recipient*, given how lazy of an answer this is (shit, I just canceled myself...). I know, older generations wanted to be actors, musicians, and athletes. I wanted to be a ninja when I was younger. But why have skills when you can just sell sex-changes and hormone therapies on TikTok – which are surprisingly popular videos.

Except the same age group in China chose astronaut as their desired career path and man... they love TikTok.

Reports say that TikTok in China doesn't show the same types of videos as in the U.S. Their highest-rated videos involve science and even patriotism. In the U.S., it is one of the most widely consumed sources of political activist content (social justice of the non-patriotic variety), and users are more likely

Ch. 7 To Be or Seem To Be, That Is The Question

to engage in activism because of Tik Tok. 77% of users report Tik Tok helped them learn about social justice and politics, nearly all Gen Z'rs have used Tik Tok, and over 60% regularly use it. Obviously, there is little possibility the Chinese government would allow dissenting political videos (Do you think TikTok allows Uighur slave camps to be shown?), and perhaps politics is what our young want to see. But what if it isn't?

We do not understand TikTok's algorithms, and many believe their videos target young Americans to sow dissent, confusion, and poor mental health. This is why the U.S. is considering banning the app.

Regardless of the potentially sinister plot, this still says something about American culture – we would rather *seem* than *be*. Irrespective of the content, producing a video that takes 5 minutes to create and receives a million views is called *success*. We expect this not only once (which is improbable enough) but repeatedly until our deathbed. Are young Americans doing anything particularly interesting? Are they disciplined and diligently working every day to reach their goal? Without researching that item at all, I can assure you – no. They just want to play the extremely low probability of lazy success and win the lottery. Marketers and companies know this, and they bombard us with that mass hallucination of easy riches to make it appear typical – it's not.

But young people can have wild dreams because little is expected of them. What are you doing?

Eddie Van Halen was noted to have practiced guitar much like my virgin friend practiced building IT servers. "When I'm home on a break, I lock myself in my room and play guitar," Van Halen told *GuitarWorld* magazine in 1981 – continuing impressive discipline even after becoming rich and famous. "If

Ch. 7 To Be or Seem To Be, That Is The Question

you're a musician, you just play until you die." He worked that hard, *and* his father was a professional musician. He *be*.

The new B.J. Novak film *Vengeance* stars himself among other faces you'd recognize but may not know their names. B.J. plays a New York journalist who travels to rural Texas to attend the funeral of an ex-fling. The deceased's family introduces themselves, including her sister Paris Shaw, the future famous filmmaker. The youngest sister joins them (and she's much prettier than the rest of the family, probably to indicate her *star power*). She's Kansas City Shaw, soon to be famous... Famous what? "A famous... celebrity."

It wouldn't be funny if it didn't ring true for our culture, at least a little bit. She does not *be*.

Sam Bankman-Fried is the MIT-educated mathematician who started the FTX and Alameda Research cryptocurrency firms. He perfected crypto arbitrage practices and became a billionaire before the age of 30. Arbitrage trading involves very sophisticated strategies that take all of the *good deals* out of the markets. He *be* brilliant – this is a fact. He also thought he was so bright he could fool everyone into believing he was a good person. He donated tens of millions (if not hundreds of millions) of dollars to Leftist charities and political campaigns and proclaimed to support effective altruism. SBF was the son of two Stanford professors and heavily involved political activists, and he worked hard to strengthen his math skills and understanding of the markets.

Effective altruism was achieved by growing FTX in order to make extremely large donations to favored political causes. He met with the Biden White House Staff (and very likely the President himself as Biden's second-largest donor), the SEC Chairman, and powerful Congressmen and women.

Ch. 7 To Be or Seem To Be, That Is The Question

He achieved billionaire status with his firms valued at roughly $30 billion at their peak. The firms actually operated at one point. They used to *be*. The SBF saga is still in progress as of this writing, but what happened is already well-known. Despite being a genius trader, he was too smart for his own good. The money flowed from investors so easily that he failed to implement safeguards and controls within his organization. These seemingly minor mistakes added up considerably over time (remember from the prior chapter about *bad luck* eventually catching up to poor practices). This led to transferring money between departments and affiliates without record, uncontrolled spending and trading, and intermingling customer funds with firm funds. Because the trading strategies were so successful early on, the organization apparently never adjusted to account for changes in the environment. Other traders copied their strategy, reducing its efficacy. They rode their own coattails of success into the dumpster as losses mounted trying to do the same old thing. He took money not his to support his failures.

The firm's executives bought over $200 million in real estate in the Bahamas and briefly lived a life that others can only dream of. SBF hired influencers to help humanize him by documenting his charitable efforts and him giving away "his" money. What happened shortly after? The businesses imploded. The executives faced legal prosecution and long-term prison sentences only three years after starting the companies. That's unfortunate...

Insiders have reported that altruism was a front to get more business and make more money. *Fake it 'til you make it*, so to speak. But he was already too good at making money. Perhaps he valued perceived virtue and wanted others to think he was a good person. He stole money to cover his mistakes, after all.

Given his political connections and having access to the world's best lawyers, he will likely receive a slap on the wrist. Not only because he's rich, but both parents are Stanford law professors, his mother was chairwoman of a Democrat Political Action Committee, his father wrote legislation for Elizabeth Warren, and his aunt sits on a council for the World Economic Forum. Knowing he is a fraud and instead of canceling his attendance, the *New York Times Deal Book Summit* interviewed SBF and gave him a microphone and venue to humanize himself after the debacle, atone for his mistakes, and place blame on others. The *NYT* later printed messages to SBF from his co-CEO to help make the case for her incompetence and relieve him of responsibility (at least in the public eye). This is not a guy who goes to jail for life.

I hope I'm wrong.

YOLO lifestyle feeds on the desire *to seem to be*. It's make-believe. Creating illusions. Living in delusions – YOLO! You spend a month's worth of earnings on renting a Lamborghini for a day just to take a photo in it or be seen around town, add 20% or more to your income when someone asks how much money you make, share only your most exciting experiences on social media, and reveal only the interesting facts and photos on your Tinder profile.

I came across a beautiful woman while trolling for a mate online. She was hot. She was also interesting. She posted photos of herself skydiving, skiing in the mountains, pub crawling downtown. Wow. I was impressed. I swiped right. We start chatting and decide to meet up. I get "catfished" … The photos were probably five years old. She tells me how

Ch. 7 To Be or Seem To Be, That Is The Question

obsessed she is with skydiving and mountain skiing. But how often can you go skydiving? She's only been once. OK... It's strange to say you're obsessed with skydiving or that it's even a hobby you've only done once, but you're nervous and trying to impress. Skiing. Which mountains does she ski on? Colorado, of course. But it has been a few years. Strike three... she's out. This told me very little about this woman except that she pads her resume well.

Is she an uninteresting person? To me, yes. She was hoping *to seem to be*, rather than just tell me who she *be*. She didn't expect someone to try to know her. Perhaps I was putting in too much effort if you know what I mean...

To make an *It's Always Sunny in Philadelphia* reference, are you *fringe class* – putting energy into donkey-brained schemes rather than just doing what is required? I have friends in their mid-30s who still scheme to meet women. They think they need an edge or some *in*. Lifts in their shoes or spending lavishly at the hottest clubs to impress other attendees. Perhaps they could try having a conversation like a human being. Who are they trying to attract with those tactics?

Would you rather retire with a million dollars, but nobody knows it, or have nothing, and people think you have a fortune? On a more immediate level, do you spend your time learning and improving your skills, or are you putting your energy toward presenting yourself as someone with more means (rents a mansion or a Lamborghini to take a few pictures in, perhaps asks attractive strangers to take a selfie with you so you seem desirable). The sharing economy provides all sorts of opportunities *to seem to be*. It was said that Tai Lopez, the social media marketing "success" personality, AirBnB'd the house he shot all of his videos in *to seem to be* more successful than he was. Another example is *Selfie Wrld*, a one-stop selfie shop where you can choose your red-carpet background to show how interesting you are, and you pay for the privilege. Or, you could go to an actual event and have something interesting to talk about.

Writers are well known for wanting *to seem to be*. This is an old trope in movies and TV – the loser trying to appear successful or interesting by calling themselves a writer, but they're really just an alcoholic. And it's real. I wanted to write and produce films with my arts degree. I worked at a restaurant as a server, had just started a business, and had recently graduated. I ran into some high school classmates and wanted to sound important. I certainly did not want to tell them I was just a waiter. Instead, I talked about how I recently *produced* an award-winning short film and was running a *startup* with another high schoolmate. I sounded like *the shit* but was just a turd struggling in near homelessness and making minimum wage. Yes, I was running a startup. Yes, our film *Tuna Lamp* won audience favorite at the Minneapolis 48-Hour Film Festival (and it was a damn good film). But I was not the success I wanted *to seem to be*. Film production was a low-budget and infrequent occurrence, and the startup never became anything. A bit more digging and they could have exposed me for the skydiving catfish fraud I was.

Some of us know what it's like to get catfished. Even if the person posts recent photos, perhaps they found the perfect angle to complement their features and to hide their true self. This is still fraud. We will hardly ever be viewed from our perfect angle – you are who you are. Do you spend hours

Ch. 7 To Be or Seem To Be, That Is The Question

taking hundreds of photos trying to find that perfect angle, or do you spend that time improving your actual self? Have you ever been reverse-catfished (the person is waaaay better than they present themselves on the profile)? That's a treat, but you're probably the catfish in that scenario.

To be is to create value; *to seem to be* is superficial. Economy is developed by value creation – the value of aggregate inputs is greater than their individual costs. Value is created when we take steel, shape it, and build a car out of the components – the car is expensive, but the raw steel is relatively cheap. But it's not about the price. A vehicle is valuable as a mode of transportation. Neither raw steel nor unassembled products can move you. Money alone cannot move you. The ability to do something you want to do but could not until now is value-creation.

Going to college can be a valuable experience. The college creates value by taking an uneducated student and imparting knowledge, logical thinking, and a framework the graduated student can use to create additional value in the world – design cars, build an engine, or edit a book.

Zero-sum transfer payments do not create value. An economy cannot survive by taking an existing item and transferring it back and forth between buyers and sellers. Think of rising housing prices or publicly traded stocks. This *seems to be* value creation because of a rising market price, but it is not.

In corporate accounting, *eliminations* are made when a company consolidates (i.e., combines) the financial statements of subsidiaries and affiliates. Eliminations are performed on intercompany transactions that do not produce net value and erase the related company sales, costs, assets, and liabilities from the consolidated performance and financial position.

An example would be two affiliates who buy and sell products from/to one another. If we did not eliminate the transactions, a company could artificially inflate its size by infinitely transferring the same product back and forth. But nothing new is created beyond the initially developed product. The same is true for our economy, and while one person or company may benefit from a sale of a pre-existing asset (house or stock), it creates no new net value. If we prepared financial statements on the economy, these transactions would be *eliminated*, if you will. (Technically speaking, GDP is the performance measure of the economy and already excludes these transactions for the same rationale).

The curious predicament of governments and central banks from around the world pumping trillions of dollars into "the economy" and producing very little economic growth illustrates my point. Since 2009, we have seen very minimal economic growth, but financial assets boomed tremendously. This results from unproductive use of funds – buying and selling financial assets and market-making. It is almost certainly why consumer price inflation did not occur during the post-2009 period; funds were injected into financial markets instead of the real economy. What we instead experienced was asset price inflation. This is the appearance of value-creation – *to seem to be*. But it does not *be*. Perhaps a few more trillion was necessary to jump-start real economic growth... Yeah right.

Interestingly, real estate and stocks are some of the only industries where "successful" businesses give away trade secrets to anyone willing to listen. Jay Gajavelli found investors through his seminars and YouTube channel, where he gave away his secrets. These are also the few industries that

Ch. 7 To Be or Seem To Be, That Is The Question

benefit from increased competition. Are you heavily invested in real estate? Your property values rise when more people join the industry and bid up the cost of homes. Same with publicly traded stocks. It pays to increase competition – more people to pass the buck to. Have you ever seen a manufacturer talk about its success and give away all of its secrets? Probably not. That's not how they get rich. Any industry whose participants can make more money by teaching you secrets than by operating successfully is worthy of extra scrutiny.

Pro-tip: Don't like your belly in photos? Use a top-down wide angle that narrows your mid-section, hides your double chin, and accentuates your cleavage. You're welcome.

Ch. 7 To Be or Seem To Be, That Is The Question
Chapter Exercise: To Seem to Be

Describe two times in which you oversold yourself or an item to another person and note if they found out the truth later:

1.   Truth Discovered: (Y / N)

2.   Truth Discovered: (Y / N)

If they found out, would you still do the same today?
(Y / N)

If they didn't find out the truth, do you know this, or are you inferring that because they never confronted you? (Y / N)

Chapter 8:

Fit-ness Matters

You want to be a pot-smoking hippie listening to Grateful Dead in a van down by the river (i.e., Van Lyfe)? Go do it. Just know that you attract what you radiate – other stoners who enjoy jam bands and unconventional living. Is that who you want? If so, you're well-aligned, and that's fantastic. I love the Grateful Dead.

In an earlier chapter, I described the 30-year-old living in his parent's basement who wants a perfect 10 woman. Do you believe perfect 10 women desire someone like that? Obviously, we are generalizing about what women want, as they could desire a variety of types. But are you realistic, or are you just hoping to win the lottery?

In a fantastic episode of *It's Always Sunny in Philadelphia*, the Gang lifts all rules at their bar to promote absolute freedom and shenanigans ensue. At first, they live their dream of sexy women coming to the bar and doing whatever they want without consequences. They love the results. However, they start to attract drug addicts and dirtbags who scare off ordinary people, and things stop working so well. They quickly learn what the values of *anything goes* ultimately attract. Frank Reynolds (played by Danny DeVito) is an excellent example of attraction. He's rich but a pure piece of shit. Who does Frank attract? The Gang (awful people by any measure), degenerates under the bridge, criminals, and he can hardly associate with anyone normal. Don't be Frank.

That's an extreme example. Closer to home, my brother is a leftist hipster who despises conservative values and refuses to engage in job upskilling outside of his employment despite being an extremely hard worker. He works in an accounting department but not as an accountant. He complained about not making enough money and earning less than the actual accountants. When I offered him my college accounting textbook, he declined. Instead, he placed the responsibility on his employer to teach him accounting. But *he* wants more money!

I showed him the path, I gave him perspective, and he refused to listen. I have no problem with this, except that he wants more. Progress is hard work. I understand why people don't want to do it, but this is called *cognitive dissonance* – wanting something but working against your own goal and feeling bad for not meeting it. If we don't want it, let's leave it be. But let's not work against ourselves or squander opportunities *when we want more*!

Rules to live by 1) There are **no** good deals (getting more than we give), 2) There are **a lot** of bad deals (we get less than we give), and 3) There are deals (we give and get equal value).

Ch. 8 Fit-ness Matters

What kind of scheme are you trying to pull if you want a *good deal*? Do you want preferable treatment or relaxed standards without putting in the effort while everyone else works harder? Or are you waiting for the world to change or for an opportunity to fall out of the sky (which is relying on luck)? These are strategies, although terrible ones. To live is to work. Get over it and put in the effort. Anything less is fraud. I provide this story for insight into the type of person my brother is. He's not a bad person, but he's a specific type of person whom many people can relate to – he doesn't want to make the investment required to obtain what he wants.

Instead, he passes the buck of responsibility to his employer who refuses to take it. Therefore, he doesn't get what he wants. Anyway, at one point while he was single, he asked how I meet quality women because he kept attracting losers. He was discouraged by the kind of women he met at dive bars, concerts, and on the apps, and I had just met a Naval Officer soon to be a Medical Doctor. My rowdy friend was equally discouraged because he had trouble attracting the type of women he desired.

You will always attract lower quality people (this is why we should not settle), not attract higher quality people, and sometimes attract the same quality person – conceptually similar to the above *deal* rules. Quality could mean anything to you – attractiveness, interests, conversation, ambition, you name it. Look in the mirror if you're unhappy with whom you attract.

It could also be how you're meeting people – Tinder is for hookups; Bumble is for relationships – so you need to know a little about marketing yourself.

For his partner search, it could have been how he was meeting people, but perhaps he was attracting people equally unwilling to put in the work and didn't like what he saw.

It's better to be discouraged and keep looking than to try to change someone who doesn't fit. You won't jive with everyone and can't change other people. Changing is tough even when you want to, so don't expect it from another for your benefit. It's nothing personal. You're just not a fit. That's OK and not a value judgment on the other person or you. The same goes for jobs – sometimes you're not a good fit. Fit-ness matters. Move on. Like a puzzle, find the right pieces, and don't mash together two pieces that don't match.

Another friend is a great guy, but he is a man's man. He uses dating apps, has a quick text conversation with women, and is unwilling to meet them unless he feels it's working. He is constantly disappointed and single.

Texting is a bad fit for building relationships. Text has limited context because the other person doesn't know your tone of voice, sarcasm, poor grammar, lack of emojis, or other nuance, all of which impact the message they receive. Perhaps your text is too wordy, or you took too long to respond. Eliminate these problems with verbal communication. I implored my friend to meet up with women as soon as it isn't creepy to ask the other person out – you need to put the investment in. The investment doesn't need to be great either – just a beer on a patio. Don't drink? Get coffee. Just do something that allows you to talk in person vs. texting. The same is true for business – don't send an email. Pick up the phone or walk in! Developing business and finding a life partner are similar in many ways.

If you need an activity on a date, walk around the lake or play some Skee-Ball. Anything more intensive is burdensome

Ch. 8 Fit-ness Matters

to do with someone who doesn't know you. Dinner can be expensive and formal. A movie provides no opportunity to get to know one another. Bowling is too much of a commitment if you don't jive. Remember: you may be great, but they don't know that. You increase your chances of finding a good match with more investments. Still, many will also not be great – so limit the initial investment in each. This is literally the same principle for finding a job or investing.

Broadly applying for jobs, you will likely have many opportunities below your skill level – the employers jump at their chance for a good deal (a more-than-qualified applicant). This doesn't mean you should ignore these companies – this is excellent interviewing experience (side note: I practiced my *about me* elevator pitch for job interviews on my Tinder dates). The more applications, the more interviews, and the more likely you will find a more fitting role. Invest in real conversations.

Fit-ness may also apply to your type of employment. If you like telling your boss to go f*** himself, self-employment is probably your best choice until you learn to control that urge. If you consistently think you are better than your coworkers or managers, finding a new company that fits your quality standard is probably best. If you can't find something better, you may be the problem.

I worked at a credit union at which I had these feelings. I was trusted with more responsibility than other employees. I objectively did more than others, and the managers held a carrot in front of me the entire way, talking about my *management potential*. Despite being better and doing more than others, I never got more. My pay wasn't higher than others, and my job satisfaction was much lower because they used my desire for more to manipulate and squeeze every ounce of productivity they could out of me. The wages were decent, and the benefits were great and improved over time. I didn't want to leave for what I believed would be a 10% raise only to lose my seniority and benefits. I settled, and they knew it.

That position was an objectively poor fit for me, but I was complacent because it wasn't bad enough. I look back and wish they would have fired me after six months – not because I wasn't good at my job or messed up, but because it wasn't a good fit and I did too little to find a better match. They knew I wasn't going to be a manager (despite often alluding to it) and did me no favors by keeping me around. I did myself no favors, either. I chased the carrot, but if I had been aware of fit-ness, I would have realized I could leave and be much better off in the right setting. Worse would have been if they had made me a manager. This only would have extended my employment and satiated me for the moment, while making it harder to eventually leave.

This bank did not care many workers slacked, were slow, or just plain terrible at their jobs. I had a quality standard, and they didn't. Companies vary. I didn't know this then and stayed much longer than I should have. Banks have different expectations from employees and varying risk tolerances for borrowers. Some banks are sub-prime lenders; others want borrowers to fit into a perfect investment-grade box. I should have searched for a bank that fit my standard. If your company lets you go, perhaps it's time to reflect on not only what you did wrong but how you fit into the organization and what to look for in your next role – the failure could easily be a function of the organization, its culture, or the position you were in. The same applies even if you've stagnated at a company. Fit-ness applies to everything in life, and that perceived injustice may instead be a blessing that forces you to take action to find the right match. I likely never would have returned to school if I caught that small-time carrot.

When a friend's car failed, he worried about buying a new one and stressed about the payment. A few years earlier, a different lender tried to charge him an exorbitant interest rate because of his supposedly lousy credit. This scared my friend from taking on debt. I was a lender at the credit union when he needed a new car, so he warned me about his credit score and expressed concerns about the expected high interest loan. He asked if I could give him a *good deal*.

His credit was solid. No blemishes, no late payments, and a great score – there was no need to give him a *good deal* because he already qualified for the best. He didn't know how the car-buying process worked, so I went shopping with him and helped him negotiate a good price on a nice VW Jetta. He was thrilled with the outcome.

Many lenders would have seen his insecurity as a weakness and pounced on him. Instead of 3%, he'd probably be paying 5%, 6%, 7% or more. That's not how I do business, and I'll talk about ethics in a later chapter. The other lender tried to convince him to take a higher interest rate loan. I had no incentive to try to screw him over on the deal, so I gave him what was fair, and he thought I got him a good deal. Regardless of the reason of the first lender, shopping around and finding a better fit paid off for my friend – which is my primary point.

We've all heard we need to shop around, but most people find personal finance uncomfortable to discuss. Credit scoring is convoluted, and the salespeople we worked with when we were young often took advantage of our naivete. Credit reports tell us in very plain and blunt language (which consumers are not accustomed to) why our score isn't perfect. Unethical salespeople will try to convince a customer with solid credit their rate is high because of that negative comment – I've been here. Except everyone has some negative remark on their report. A score over 730 is usually considered great credit, and most loan rates are based primarily, if not solely, on the score – beware of someone convincing you otherwise.

As stated earlier, my dad worked most of his life as a sole proprietor. He did this because 1) it was his way of making more money by working harder, and 2) he could not stand working for dumb managers. Nearly everyone is dumb in his eyes, and therefore, self-employment is a better fit.

Around the mid-2010s, my parents were still paying a 10% interest rate on a mortgage they received in the early 90s. Mortgage rates were under 4% at this time, and they could have achieved significant savings of a few hundred dollars per month by refinancing, so I asked my dad why he hadn't. Apparently, he tried to refinance several years earlier, and the bank wouldn't approve him because he was self-employed and his credit wasn't great. What was his score? He didn't know. He had only tried one lender and assumed all others would tell him the same thing. Had he tried a credit union or searched for a bank that caters to the self-employed? No. He also stubbornly refused to acknowledge that banks have varying standards or that times may differ from when he last tried many years earlier – quantitative easing changed lending. He learned something once with one institution, failed, and never reconsidered that the times changed, or perhaps the failure was a function of the institution, not him. He paid a 10% rate and several thousands of dollars more in interest until he fully repaid the loan years later.

Ch. 8 Fit-ness Matters

Another friend refinanced his two vehicle loans at the suggestion of his personal banker. He was paying 3% and 4% on two loans, and his banker advised that he could save money on interest payments by consolidating them into a single 5% loan. This made sense to my friend and his banker because 5% is lower than the combined 7% of the other loans. But is it? No. It's actually much worse because the appropriate method is to use a weighted-average interest rate. The concept of weighted-average rates is crucial for bankers to understand. Did this banker not understand this concept, or was he maliciously trying to meet his sales goals?
It doesn't matter because this terrible advice nonetheless impacted my friend who followed it.

By consolidating his loans at 5%, my friend paid $500 more each year in interest expense. He will lose much more if he continues to work with incompetent advisors. I know, this isn't an exciting million-dollar deal. These are decisions that every day people need to consider.

Know where you stand. If you accept shit deals, you're going to receive shit deals. Do not settle. If you are quality and demand quality, you'll obtain quality. But you will still have to work to find it.

Pro-tip: If you are shit, your deals will still be shit.

Chapter Exercise: Connections

List the last three connections you made with strangers and score the personal connection from 1 to 10 (10 being the best).

1. Score _____

2. Score _____

3. Score _____

Total score: _____

Are you satisfied with the results? (Y / N)

Try this again in a few weeks to monitor your progress.

BONUS CHAPTER:
THE POWER BELLY

The *Power Belly* is not the *dad-bod*. The *Power Belly* is a belly so intrusive it encroaches on your personal space during conversation. You know this feeling. Their face is at a socially-appropriate distance, but their belly is nearly touching you. It leaves no room for Jesus. You feel powerless in its gravitational pull and are compelled to do its bidding.

Chapter Exercise: Power Belly

Measure your waist circumference. It's not big enough to be powerful. Go eat a box of Twinkies.

Chapter 9:

Opportunity

Beware of the curse of success: Opportunity comes in waves. I have been unemployed for a period and then received three offers within a week or so of each other. I have also been stuck in a lousy job for a year or two hearing nothing from outside employers, then boom – three job offers at significantly higher salaries. This is entirely anecdotal, but many people report a similar phenomenon.

When I met my wife (aka *forever wife*), I had other opportunities with women around the same time – I chose wisely. I have not always chosen wisely. It is tough to choose wisely. It is effortless to settle. No matter what you value, settling is never a good choice – this is so vague it's almost meaningless, so please read on.

If you have multiple job offers, take time to dig into each a little more. Perhaps you like one, but the pay isn't as high as another – now you have leverage to request a higher salary, bigger bonus potential, more time off, or another perk you're interested in. Feel free to get creative. The real opportunity here is to delay accepting an offer and to dig in.

If you leap quickly into any offer, you may not have options at other companies later if the new position is not everything you dreamed it would be or how the manager described it. Perhaps the money isn't worth the work, or the boss is a prick – problems are potentially infinite – dig into *why you should* take a job, pick a partner, or associate with friends. Express concern for yourself by asking more questions of the employers. Consider what you have or haven't liked in previous roles and ask your prospective employers about those factors. To not dig deeper is to settle. Digging in is implicitly part of the negotiation.

Some people are so afraid of negotiating or losing an offer they accept anything to avoid conflict. Do not be this person. Negotiating can lose you the offer, but if you have in-demand skills, likability, and a decent track record, you will have another one (and perhaps you can ease off the pressure a bit next time). Do not be afraid of gaining this valuable experience even if it costs you one offer.

My worst jobs moved very quickly to lock me in. My first interview goes well; they tell me they'll be in touch in a week or two, but suddenly, they want to meet again tomorrow and the next day, and boom – the offer comes within a week. Corrupt companies may do this to stop you from interviewing elsewhere. They know what they want, you fit what they want, and they won't allow another employer to make a better offer. Stop and think: How desperate are they if they can move this quickly? This doesn't mean not to take it, but beware and ask a few more questions – deliberately slow down the process.

Ch. 9 Opportunity

Sometimes, an opportunity requires you to take a step back to move forward. When I left my landscaping company, I gave up the most money I had ever made to attempt to find an equally well-paying role that didn't require 80-hour weeks.

My earnings over the period with ($ deviation from 2015 / cumulative $ deviation):

2015: $70,000 ($0 / $0)

2016: $25,000 (-$45,000 / -$45,000)

2017: $55,000 (-$15,000 / -$60,000)

2018: $75,000 (+$5,000 / -$55,000)

You could view this as me giving up $60,000 in the first two years (opportunity cost) to surpass my prior earnings by the third year. This has since paid off immensely as I enjoy my work and life balance, have covered all monetary losses, and have far exceeded what I hoped for in salary. To provide additional perspective (without giving away too much), I rejected an offer a few years ago for a sales position that would pay a six-figure base salary plus 1% commissions on the loans I originate (if I originate $100 million in loans, I receive $1,000,000), a car allowance, and many other perks. I did not pursue that opportunity because money is not my primary concern.

My "success" is anecdotal and partly a function of my industry – banking can pay well. A corporate financial analyst was another potential career path that wouldn't have been as fruitful in the same amount of time, no matter how good I was. Whereas investment banking, private equity, or working on Wall Street trading stocks or bonds could have provided much higher income, but my problem with 80-hour weeks wouldn't have been solved. Your success is a function of the industry and company in which you work. This doesn't mean it controls your destiny, but it is a constraint. If you're trying to make six figures, a retail or service-industry job will never get you there. Those supposedly well-paid manager positions are not as well-paying as you think and are rare because you compete with many others for limited openings.

Perhaps you want to leave your full-time job to start a business or become self-employed – you value doing your own thing more than the time, the long days, and hard work. From a purely financial perspective, you must understand your opportunity cost, your break-even, and the economic nuance of running a business (start-up investment, how much to charge, minimum revenue required to break even, the minimum number of units needed to hit that revenue, minimum revenue to pay yourself a living wage, how long it will take to hit that point, can you survive in the meantime, can you afford to half-ass this?) This will be a step back until you're operating sufficiently.

The next step is to make up for the income you gave up during the start-up period in which you worked for less than you could have doing something else (and for less than minimum wage in many cases).

Most people don't understand a simple truth of entrepreneurship: There are only two ways to grow a business. (i) Steal market share from competitors, or (ii) Be part of a growing industry with ample new opportunities you can retain a portion of for yourself. Many overly optimistic entrepreneurs enter mature (low-growth) industries by undercutting the competition and stealing business from current operators. These undercutters are very likely taking excessive risk to entice buyers by offering reduced prices. This is why mergers and acquisitions occur in mature industries – buying a book of business from someone else is preferred to undercutting to grow. By participating in a booming industry, many of those problems are eliminated – you may grow by default with strong margins because there are not enough companies to fulfill demand.

Finding a job is conceptually similar. The more tangible skills required, the fewer competitors vying for the same role. An industry or function experiencing high growth is more likely to accept an outsider. With both conditions, high growth and tangible skills, (think software development, coding, or other IT-related careers), good opportunities will knock on your door. Your industry is a dominant constraint.

Many small businesses don't close up because they're losing money. With owner-operators, likely, they're just not making *enough*. What's enough? That depends on the owner and their other options.

My tile guy is skilled. He and three other guys show up on a job site each day, and he charges $3,000 for roughly a whole week of work for all of them (labor only). After payroll, he is probably personally grossing around $1,000. That's $52,000 per year if he doesn't take any vacations and has job after job lined up. That also doesn't include his self-employment taxes and benefits, the portions which employees don't typically pay for, so he's probably making the equivalent of less than $40,000/year if he were working for someone else. Not a terrible salary for a 25-year-old, and he's making more than I did when I was his age, even with a degree, but he's accepting all of the risks of the business. His dad, who is probably 50 years old, works with him. $40,000 with few benefits at 50 years old is a tough life. At 65, it will be even more challenging, and so will tiling. Perhaps this company is not charging enough, or that's where the market is, and this is what they need to charge to keep a full schedule – i.e., it's a reality of the industry that they (the individual company) cannot change. They must give up some jobs or close their business entirely if they want something different. I respect what they're doing enough not to negotiate with them either – I know they're not ripping me off.

There is nothing wrong with what they're doing. This is not a judgment against them or their incomes. If you run a business, you need to know your competitive advantage. You should also strive to understand your advantage as an employee. Whether your competitive advantage is being the lowest cost, hardest working, or best quality, you must ask yourself if the answer is acceptable. Being a low-cost provider is not objectively flawed, but it is if you are above average quality. I've had many co-workers rationalize that their lower- than-average salary gives them an advantage when the economy weakens. That's great if the wage is the employer's only consideration, but what if the hardest working is who they want to keep when they cut the fat? Now you've been working for less for no reason. Being above-average quality is great if you charge above-average prices or are allowed leniency with your schedule to meet your standard. Rushing above-average quality for cheap is only a good deal for the customer, and it's only acceptable if you understand the *good deal* you are providing them (and the *bad deal* for you).

The *contractor's triangle* is a great tool to understand your advantage, even if you're not a contractor. The triangle consists of three components: cost, time, and quality, and there is a tradeoff between the three. The only way to do any project well and quickly is at a high cost. The quality will decline if you want your project done quickly and cheaply. Low cost and

Ch. 9 Opportunity

high quality will take a long time. There is always a constraint. Likewise, there is always a constraint outside of the *contractor's triangle*. Know the conditions of your situation.

I'm not saying anyone should quit if their advantage is not what they desire or the constraints of the situation limit their discretion and income. The correct action depends on your values, but understand that quitting is OK. Do not beat yourself against a brick wall; question your fit-ness when you're not getting what you want. Quitting has a bad connotation, but it's entirely acceptable when you're in a lousy deal, are a bad fit, or are just not making the progress you desire. We all make poor decisions at some point. Tech companies have rebranded quitting as *pivoting*. I have *pivoted* many times in my life. I received minimal direction for my choices and failed to ask why for what I was doing for much of it; therefore, I had to learn from my mistakes. I caught a lot of flak from my family and friends for divorcing my first wife after leaving the Air Force and losing everything. I barely bounced back, failed to reflect on my mistakes, jumped into another opportunity, and married someone who wasn't a good fit again. I got divorced again, lost everything, and caught a bunch of flak again. This is why people don't want you to quit –you can get caught in a failure loop again and again and again. I was in a failure loop for years with relationships and jobs. Failure can be devastating or help you learn (i.e., resilience or, better yet, antifragility).

The *sunk cost fallacy* is a critical concept in finance. This refers to the belief that something has ongoing value because of what has been invested in it. In business, this could be research and development costs of a new prescription drug or computer software in which you've invested heavily. The same could be true for any business. Do you continue to invest because of the amount already invested, even if the market has shifted?

Bad leaders double down on poor decisions and continue to invest despite the reduced returns. Alternatively, it could be a government policy with unintended consequences outweighing the benefits. Managers often refuse to acknowledge failures, making this a critical concept in business school. Employees also fall for the fallacy. At the credit union, I didn't want to leave after putting in so much effort to build a knowledge base of the company, its culture, and its processes. Six more months and they'll promote me, went through my mind every six months.

A personal relationship also feels like an investment. You may spend years with someone only to find out they're not the person with whom you initially fell in love. In relationships, the *sunk cost fallacy* is experienced by staying with a partner because of your history, not because of the expectations of your happy future together. If you've put seven years into the relationship, but it's going downhill, you need to continue with it, right? No. That's the fallacy at work. You must view all decisions on a go-forward basis. **This does not relieve us of the responsibility of doing what is in our power to make a decision work.** Still, it does mean it is OK to quit, *eh hem*, pivot when future expectations are worse by sticking to the current decision.

Do not mistake this as meaning we should quit and do nothing – giving up entirely is not an option. We must move forward with the next best alternative. Resilience is only built by failure, and we cannot reach our potential if we've never pushed our limits. A former employer of mine called this concept *failing forward*.

Ch. 9 Opportunity

I reflected heavily preceding the last divorce on what I wanted not just in a partner but in life, my career, everything. To build the life I wanted, I needed a partner whose values aligned with mine. A partner who supports me in spirit and actions. This is not a pardon nor indictment of my prior wives – we were not a good fit, and we failed to see it. Fit-ness matters, bad deal or not. I also left many jobs and industries. I also caught a lot of shit for bouncing around, and I deserved it. But not any longer.

I became conscious of my prior mistakes when making new decisions. If you fail, you must reflect on your mistakes, no matter how exogenous the cause of failure appears, and move forward. It's never too late to develop the life you desire. I was almost 30 before I started questioning *why*. I finally developed self-esteem that helped me create a standard for what I wanted – no more settling. I have more than made up for my mistakes.

In my twenties, my family worried I was just jumping from one opportunity to the next, blindly believing the *grass is always greener* and never taking the reins of my life. They were right about me, but I have zero regrets and have gained much satisfaction from these changes. But change takes time, and even after being made, changes will rarely yield immediate results.

I have now found someone who challenges me to improve and brings me more happiness than I could have imagined. In material terms, I lost a lot of possessions in divorce. I had to take several steps back initially to move to the next level. My *forever wife's* support helps me progress faster than I could on my own. Does your partner put up or knock down barriers to the life you want? You can skip the heartache and lost homes by learning from my mistakes and following a values and fitness forward approach.

Reflect, step back, and charge forward, time and time again.

Ch. 9 Opportunity

Chapter Exercise: Dream position

Read the job description of your dream position. List the three primary quantitative requirements and score your fit- ness to the related requirement on a scale of 1 to 10 (10 being 100% matching.). *(For example, a position requires 5 years of related experience, and you have 4 years. You would score this an "8")*

1. Your Score: _____

2. Your Score: _____

3. Your Score: _____

Chapter Exercise: What will it take?

Jobs typically do not require applicants to meet 100% of requirements. For any requirement not scored an "8" or higher (80% matching), detail what is necessary to hit at least 80%.

1.

2.

3.

How long will it take to meet these requirements? _____

Do you need to upskill, or is it a waiting game to obtain the number of years of experience desired by the employer?

_____

Should this stop you from applying? (Y / N)

Chapter 10:

Personality-Driven Success

A leader is strong-willed, unwavering, innovative, and charismatic. You look at someone with those characteristics and say, "They must be successful."

The person saying that doesn't know many successful people. Personality-driven success doesn't exist except for motivational speakers and actors.

But what about sales? No. Many people incorrectly think of sales as a used-car con man saying, with finger pistols blasting away, "Hey, good lookin'. You deserve to drive home in this used Fiat!." That is not sales, and anyone doing that sucks at their job.

Actual sales is about asking questions and digging for answers, not talking. Definitely not *smooth talking*. Take an opportunity to meet with a few salespeople to see the differences in what a good and lousy salesperson does.

I learned a great sales lesson working at a restaurant. We were re-vamping our website and called three companies for quotes. Two wanted to meet face-to-face. One just emailed us

Ch. 10 Personality-driven Success

a quote for $4,000, and the only question they asked us was if we needed anything else. Despite being the lowest price, we did not select this company – they had no idea what we wanted. Of the two we met, one woman told us how great her company was, all the services they provide, and all the SEO (search engine optimization) we needed. Hardly did she ask us any questions. All the guy did from the last company was ask questions. What did *we* want, who are *we* attracting, what functions do *we* desire?

The woman was charismatic and well-spoken, telling us all the right things about her capability. The man was straight-faced and unemotional, but **his questions showed concern for our business**. His quote was more than twice as much as the first company and the highest of all three, but guess who we chose?

Just like you won't meet many quality partners by texting, we never gave the emailed quote company a chance, either. We chose the company with the most concern for our business, and received a great product.

The ability to probe to the heart of an issue with meaningful questions requires concern for the customer, a level of intelligence, and knowledge of a subject. There are more sophisticated sales jobs than others. Car sales, while a great profession, doesn't require much expert knowledge. An intelligent person can train up in less than a day for these jobs and do *good enough* (yes, the grammar is off there, but you understand the point). The tactics used in these roles (which deal with consumers) differ from business-to-business sales. I am not knocking car salesmen just because they are relatively unsophisticated – this is just a fact, not a value judgment. I love buying a new car. I've done it several times, and the feeling of signing the paperwork, grabbing the keys, and driving that baby home the first time is awesome. My car buying experience started with a brand-new $10,000 110- horsepower manual transmission Hyundai Accent hatchback from Jim Click Hyundai in Tucson, financed by USAA at 5% after arriving at Davis-Monthan Air Force Base in 2007. I loved that car. I remember very few experiences with as much detail, and I would love to help others create similar memories.

The other defining characteristics of strong salespeople are their resilience and whether they can be trusted. These may sound like personality traits, but they are learned skills. You can learn resilience by leaving your comfort zone and gain trust by showing concern for the customer's problem. In the earlier chapter, resilience (or lack thereof) is illustrated by my friend and dad shopping for loans. Resilience allows us to experience more opportunities to find a good fit. This could be a sales customer, a partner, a job, a company, a car dealership, a lender, and more. Settling is the opposite of resilience.

I was the salesman when my successful friend and I started an IT consulting company. My friend pressed me on my ability to handle rejection – I couldn't. He wanted me to go to a Target store and try starting a conversation with a random person. I gave him every excuse I could muster of why that's different than sales. It's not different. Conceptually, building resilience and the ability to ask good questions is what sales is. Having a conversation with a random person is how to strengthen that muscle. While we didn't become millionaires as expected, this was a great introduction to building resiliency and finding my weaknesses. Over time, I learned the value of asking questions and speaking less.

The night I met my forever wife, I was out with a buddy at a brewery trying to relax during the most harrowing period of

Ch. 10 Personality-driven Success

my life. I had returned to school for my finance degree, working an internship, and at the tail-end of a failed marriage. Trying to balance this was more challenging than when running the landscaping business. I may not have been working 80-hour weeks, but I was pulled in a dozen different directions, causing mental exhaustion and burnout. Still being in school, I told myself I couldn't leave my now ex-wife because we owned a house, I took a massive pay cut returning to school, had limited savings, and had no capacity for more stress. So, my ex and I were still married and living together. I was living a lie, but divorce would postpone my graduation due to the energy required. I was on a strict schedule to graduate on time, so there was no way to ease the burden.

The brewery had long picnic-style tables with multiple groups at each one. There was a small opening, and we asked if we could squeeze in, which my forever wife and her friend allowed. Somehow, we all started chatting and connecting on being veterans – she was Navy, I was Air Force, and my buddy was a Marine. Her friend was very much excluded from the conversation as a civilian, even though I was kicking my buddy under the table to give her some attention. Because I was extremely unhappy in my situation and trying to hide the fact I'm married, I was very proactive with my questions – as simple as can you tell me about that? Luckily, she enjoyed talking. We chatted for a few hours; I was incredibly impressed and asked for her phone number. Here we are today.

She knew very little about me and had no idea I was hitting on her. She appreciated the interest I showed with my questions, which helped her feel comfortable giving me her number. It wasn't because I was some suave gentleman smelling of Axe Body Spray or impressive in anything that evening (my buddy and I lost a game of cornhole against the girls, so if anything, I was at a disadvantage). I never bought her a drink. I simply expressed interest in her life – the same feature the web developer showed for the restaurant.

Her trust in me and our relationship thrived because of my follow-through on commitments to improving her life, and the same from her to me. Complete trust was not earned in one conversation but developed over time through more interactions. I didn't get to marry a medical doctor by being a total jabroni.

(NOTE: I was a piece of shit. Do not follow my lead on being married and going out to meet women. I do not condone this – I was a loser in the wrong place, miserable, and trying to find happiness any way I could. Those are not excuses for poor behavior. Had I been capable of examining my values and planning appropriately, I wouldn't have been in my failed marriage in the first place and participating in nonsense. Learn from my mistake here. And for the record, my friend lost us that cornhole game against the girls)

Genuine concern for another with follow-through on commitments are skills required *to be*. Suaveness, cologne, scheming to meet a partner or obtain a job, or making commitments you cannot keep is to *seem to be*. This is equally true in business. Well-paying jobs require more than superficial traits. There is no personality trait that will make you successful.

One caveat to this is that personalities need to jive – fit- ness matters. Nobody wants to work with an obnoxious salesman or coworker. Despite the dynamic duo of Riggs and Murtaugh (or, my favorite, Shawn and Gus) sometimes working out, we are attracted to people like us. We want a partner who will

Ch. 10 Personality-driven Success

make us better, but we don't want someone who challenges us on everything. If you're an extrovert and with an introvert, you will clash when you want to leave the house and vice-versa. This doesn't mean it won't work, but be aware of the challenges you will face. Personality can lose you a deal but will never solely make a deal.

Trying to actively listen or appear engaged, many of us will finish other people's sentences during conversations. I am very guilty of this. This isn't automatically a bad thing, but it puts you in a position of assuming to know what people are talking about. Assuming is the critical problem here. Many intelligent or well-informed people are thoughtful listeners but put themselves in a position to be taken advantage of. Schemers prey on their assumptions about terms or phrases, and there are a lot of schemers in the corporate world. I illustrated earlier that people have different concepts of the same term, and we often bring our own definitions or connotations to conversations. Imagine two people talking about freedom, where one's concept is land, funds, and time to develop said land into a vision, and the other's concept of freedom is owning nothing. Have you ever argued with someone for 20 minutes over the same terms, only to find out you are discussing different problems? This confusion can happen in a work setting, inhibiting your ability to dig deeply enough to solve problems. Legal agreements provide key definitions for this very reason. It is why I provide key term definitions in this book.

In banking, my weakest commercial customers have expressed their "strong" performance based on various financial ratios or other calculations they came up with, only for me to find out they are breaching the terms of their agreement. I matched my calculation to the loan agreement (which they signed and agreed to) while they created their own calculation based on the most favorable interpretation for the ratios – but we are using the same terminology. Perhaps they add back significant expenses to their cash flow that are not allowed per the agreement, and they calculate their ratios based on this extraordinarily favorable and loose definition. You would think the same calculations would be used consistently, but there is almost no consistency. Borrowers use this fact to their advantage at the bank's expense (savvy bankers also use this ambiguity by crafting new definitions to get their weakest loans approved).

Is it fair if the bank accepts the incorrect covenant calculation over many periods but then changes course and calls a customer in default? The courts say no because an expectation was created for the borrower that this was acceptable. The banker's repeated acceptance of inappropriate behaviors and violated terms essentially re- writes the original terms of the agreement, no matter what was signed. They now have limited recourse. It is the banker's responsibility to perform due diligence and hold borrowers accountable (many do not because they want the borrower to stay happy and not look for another bank – an example of excessive risk-taking as a competitive advantage). Nobody sympathizes with a dogshit banker. Beware of your assumptions.

A friend recently applied for Department of Veteran's Affairs disability benefits. He suffered a concussion from service that still impacts his life. When he told his family and peers, they told him he was not disabled because he was walking around and appeared to be doing fine. Their image of a disabled vet is a wheelchair-bound amputee, not a guy with observable physical function holding a decent job. Fortunately

Ch. 10 Personality-driven Success

for my friend, he didn't listen to them and filed for disability. He is now paid $700 per month for the rest of his life because the VA's definition of disabled matched the impact he incurred, not the assumed definition or image commonly held of disabled people. Unfortunately for that friend, he missed out on over $100,000 in payments by holding the same assumptions as his peers for more than a decade after separation. This stopped him from filing a claim earlier, and the VA does not back pay.

The VA's definition only requires a service-connected injury or diagnosis that continues to impact your life. They provide varying degrees of benefits depending on the severity of the disability – e.g., the amputee gets more benefits than someone with long-lasting athlete's foot. If you believe you have a service-connected disability, visit VA.gov/disability for more details or to file for benefits.

Assumptions are for suckers.

There is a meme that states: Before you marry someone: 1) Listen to them eat a bowl of cereal, 2) Ask them which side of the bed they sleep on, 3) Watch them brush their teeth, 4) Make sure you are temperature compatible, 5) Survive one cold and flu season at a minimum.

Pro-tip: No matter how charismatic you are, your partner will hate you if you chomp loudly on a bowl of cereal. I learned this the hard way...

Chapter Exercise: Resilience

Detail two instances where you failed in the last 5 years and note if you have since re-attempted the same.

1.   Re-attempted: (Y / N)

2.   Re-attempted: (Y / N)

Is the fear of failure holding you back? (Y / N)

Chapter Exercise: Questions

Detail the last three questions you asked someone.

1.

2.

3.

Were you satisfied with their response? (Y / N)

Do you need to dig deeper? (Y / N)

Chapter 11:

The Working Class Works too Hard.

I learned how to work from my dad. You probably learned from yours as well. My dad taught me to take my job seriously and think like a business owner – what would I do if I owned the company I worked for? Work hard, waste no time, and push others to increase efficiencies were the fundamental values instilled. This may have benefited his generation when he was younger, but not any longer. Corporations are not meritocracies and solving problems the business faces isn't value-added unless the top of the house has identified them first. Companies say they want *leaders* and *entrepreneurs* for low-to-mid-level employees, but my experience shows this is all coded language and means nothing like what it sounds.

If a company wants *leaders*, it means they don't want you. Leadership is a qualitative trait that is ill-defined in most settings. Companies that desire *leaders* are looking for i) culture drivers, ii) order followers with no ability to think for themselves, or iii) their buddies (not you). Very likely, it is all three. If it's something more tangible, why not just say it?

Companies that talk about the importance of leadership tend to promote terrible managers. How do the managers obtain their role? Usually nepotism. It's why you think your boss sucks – they probably do. When promotion time comes, who will get promoted to manager first, the uber-productive competent worker with no connections or the unproductive worker with super connections? The answer is clear if we think back to that underqualified banker whose *Daddy* called the department head for her job. Managers typically do not produce – they manage producers – therefore, the company will choose the unproductive person for management over the productive person. In other words, leaders get promoted because they're useless as contributors. Why lose a solid contributor by promoting them? If the unqualified nepotistic hire's productivity was a material concern, they wouldn't have been hired, or they would have gone through the standard application process. But they didn't. This doesn't apply to all companies, but it is rampant in the private sector, particularly in large organizations.

If a requirement for a position is leadership, what does that mean? It sounds like they can disqualify you for any reason. And they can. Adding *leadership* to your resume after seeing it in a job description makes you look like a total jabroni to the hiring manager, and they will remain unconvinced. The *leader* they're looking for is the connected employee they've already identified. Calling yourself a leader is solely to *seem to be*, and they know it.

Entrepreneurship, on the other hand, is the requirement they are going to i) work you hard, ii) pay you less than the market

Ch. 11 The Working Class Works Too Hard

rate, and iii) you're willing to put up with it, which is what entrepreneurship usually is when starting a business. My family thrives in this environment, initially praised, but we never make the money we deserve after giving them what they ask for. We do not understand what the companies actually want – for us to work harder for less. But praise doesn't pay rent.

This relates to the working class because your family never taught you how to spot corporate double-speak. The language is constantly evolving, and corporate jobs are a niche of the job market that most people are just not part of, especially the working class. My family had no corporate employees in it. We hear terms like leadership and entrepreneur, and we think of how smart we are and how we could succeed if we were just given the opportunity – which is probably true. They remind us of true leaders who forged paths and the entrepreneurs who pulled themselves up by their bootstraps. If you're a combat veteran, you remember how often you exhibited authentic leadership and believe that is what they want. These companies strive to elicit these images but without any substance. Your assumptions about these terms or what your company means by them impact how you react when you hear them. They know this. Your assumptions about the words are why they use them without ever having to follow through.

Hearing these terms, you think you will be rewarded for innovation and finding solutions to problems or inefficiencies that management wasn't aware of. Management sees your over-eagerness as weakness and exploits it. They use this opportunity to pile on work. Disproportionately more work than others. They found their *Pareto's Principle* 20%'r.

Ch. 11 The Working Class Works Too Hard

Pareto's Principle: 20% of the employees do 80% of the work. Or, 80% of employees do jack-shit. Anyone working in corporate America can tell you it is real, and it's often discussed in business school.

80%'rs know how corporate America works: be well-connected and wait your turn.

Working-class people sell themselves on how hard they work. Working hard isn't the only factor; it's not even a primary factor. If it was, Pareto's Principle wouldn't ring true, and 80% of people wouldn't contribute less than their relative proportion of the workforce. So, what else is there?

I met another friend while working at a credit union branch. He was going to school for Business Management, he was the worst employee I had ever met, and he struggled with basic arithmetic (not a great quality for someone in finance). However, he was an incredible conversationalist and could talk to anyone. Customers loved him. I learned a lot by watching him converse with people. But I always thought he was going to get fired. He never did. He was a great guy. He wasn't connected, but he was very well-liked. After graduating college, he found another job and put in his two weeks' notice with our employer. Within a few days, he calls me for advice on a "once in a lifetime opportunity" but will need to skip out on his last week of work – this is not surprising given his awful productivity. I tell him he should work his remaining shifts. He doesn't overthink it and never shows up again. He went on a cross-country ATV trip with his buddies and built a long-lasting and fruitful career with his new employer.

The day he didn't show up, our manager explained to our team his call to her (same as mine). Rather than wishing him

Ch. 11 The Working Class Works Too Hard   147

well and moving past the unfortunate circumstances of him skipping out, she states, "He doesn't care about us." I heard how former employees "don't care about us" over and over from various managers when anyone quit. That company promoted and hired *leaders*, and I have never experienced a company with higher employee turnover.

Strong, ethical, working-class people would have stayed and finished their two weeks. Is that the right thing? I don't know. But I know my buddy went on a great trip and never regretted it, and I wouldn't have under the same circumstance.

A new movement calls for workers to act your wage – don't put in the effort the employer isn't paying you for, or don't give the employer a *good deal*, as I like to say. This is a fair movement, but it ignores the fact that sometimes your salary is a function of your potential, not just your present output.

Very few large organizations will fire you for underperforming. They are afraid to fire people. More than likely, they will put up with you perpetually. They may never give you more (promotions, meaningful raises, or anything else you want), but they will tolerate you. My rule is that any lazy person can last two years in any corporate job if they don't mess up too badly. Your first year is spent getting up to speed. Your manager realizes their mistake of hiring you in months 12-18 and maybe puts you on a performance plan. They then give you another six or so months to coast to your two-year mark before they let you go – if they have the balls to let you go. Companies don't want to fire employees, and you will likely never be fired. However, you will be on the chopping block when layoffs inevitably occur (which could happen before the two-year mark if the economy tanks). This applies to large organizations.

Ch. 11 The Working Class Works Too Hard

Do not slack at a small company – they will fire you.

I very much believe in doing the right thing, but my idea of what is right has changed meaningfully over time. In my twenties, I worked much harder than I do now. If I was given a task, I did it, no questions asked. My former supervisors say I was the best worker they ever had and one that never needs to be managed. Customers at the restaurant I worked for asked if I owned the place. I took pride in that. I don't any longer.

Being the best worker meant the company received a *good deal* from me. Was I rewarded? Not with meaningful money or promotions. Why promote your best contributor? 80%'rs know this. This is why you don't get promoted, and most managers suck.

The private sector is not a meritocracy.

Finance teaches about the problem of agency – managers are self-serving pricks who will do what's best for themselves always. They do not do what's best for the organization unless incentivized. Finance solves this by structuring pay and incentives to encourage the right behaviors. If you are a great worker – the manager's golden goose – what motivates them to promote you? You'll quit? Who cares. You don't work for them any longer if they promote you, and it's the same outcome if you leave. I repeat: what incentive do they have to promote you? Managers do not do what's best for the organization just because.

Only working-class people with an entrepreneurial mindset do what's best for an organization *just because*.

This is not to say you should be a self-serving prick. You cannot afford to be one. You'll be figured out quickly and

Ch. 11 The Working Class Works Too Hard

shunned. You don't have Daddy to call the head of the department to buy your next management job for you.

This is also not to say you should slack. Studies confirm that moderately competent, well-liked employees get promoted the fastest. Determine the quality and performance standard, provide that, and be well-liked.

Studies also suggest that tit-for-tat is generally the best strategy in any situation. Tit-for-tat is the idea that you ask me for something, and I ask for something from you (or, in Game Theory, cooperating until the other party defects). My first manager in commercial banking taught me to keep a list of what I want from every borrower. You don't ask them for everything you want whenever you want it. Be patient. When the borrower requests something from you, you oblige and ask for something from them of equal value.

For example, a Borrower has a line of credit renewing soon. You need to bump up their pricing but cannot until the loan matures, so you wait. The borrower requests their line of credit to be renewed, plus an increase in size. This is a prime opportunity. You perform your analysis, determine the appropriate increase, and inform them of the good news: you received approval, and it will only cost them SOFR + 250bps and a $50,000 fee – last year's price plus compensation for the renewal and the increase. And you meet your goals.

This does not mean to bend them over a barrel. Tit-for-tat should be roughly matched. Do not try to get a good deal.

Terrible business advice states that you should never leave money on the table in any negotiation, meaning if someone is a sucker, in a pickle, or just plain willing to pay more, always try to haggle the most from them. This goes against the tit- for-tat strategy and the research. If you fight for every last penny, you will be known as the defector (and your behavior will catch up with you). Defectors eventually lose. When someone is down and you bend them over a barrel, they will remember and do the same to you when you need something and tell their network the same. Is this the kind of life you want: constantly screwing and being screwed? Living on high one day and losing it all the next? That is what that lifestyle breeds. It is unsustainable or at least unrewarding. Do not do business with people like this. Even if you win today, they will try to screw you in the future and have no desire for what is fair, ever. If you must work with someone like this, fight hard and walk away from an unfair deal.

On the flip side, not negotiating is the absolute worst strategy, and you will be the one bent over a barrel time and time again, never moving forward. There is a happy medium, which is to know what is fair, demand fairness, and build a human connection and reciprocal relationship. Give and take equal value. But if they screw you, you will hit back. This only applies if you are being reasonable, which is difficult to determine because fairness is very subjective.

If you request a promotion from your manager, they will very likely simultaneously turn down your request and ask for more from you. Do you accept more responsibility if they just rejected you? The correct answer depends on how fair you believe your manager to be. Is your manager constantly seeking a better deal from you and giving nothing in return, or did they surprise you with a solid bonus and pay raise last year and are thus likely to reward you if you play ball?

People think of negotiations beginning at trading. Trading is when an offer is made, and you go back and forth regarding terms and amounts – the quintessential tit-for-tat moment. However, negotiations begin long before this point. Negotiations start the moment we sit down with a

Ch. 11 The Working Class Works Too Hard

prospective employer, customer, or partner. It begins when we discuss our desires, problems, solutions, values, and skills. Your narrative is a significant component of the negotiation, just as is showing concern for yourself and the employer by asking meaningful questions.

Your narrative is the first step of the negotiation, so build a good one. If a prospective employer asks why you're looking for a new job and you tell them your current employer is screwing you on pay, you're making a terrible impression. This new employer doesn't know you. Perhaps you're getting screwed because you just suck. They do not know you. You increase your perceived risk. These comments create uncertainty in their anticipated returns from your labor and reduce the offer they will make you.

Another critical component of the narrative is salary discussions. I never give my salary in a job interview. Instead, I may allude to how much money I make – my condo downtown, the home I own in the hot area of town, my wife is a medical doctor. This tells them I am no buster, and others value what I provide, but not enough information for them to say, "We'll give you your current salary plus $1,000."

Managers care how much others value you. I've worked with borrowers who management hated until they discovered another bank was interested in them. They drop their pricing to give that once-hated customer a good deal, yet their best customers continue to pay more. The same happens with employees. When a company thinks they're your only offer, they try to screw you, but suddenly someone else values you more, and your worth goes up for them. This is linked to power – they thought they had power over you when they were the only offer, but now they have less power. Stupid games. Pay a person their expected contribution (i.e., value; a fair deal).

Ch. 11 The Working Class Works Too Hard

Walk away if you can't make a balanced deal. Also, never lie about having another offer. Their power multiplies after calling your bluff.

I never make the job search about money. Money is overly rational. Counterintuitively, relaying money's importance to you is the worst message to send. You are a human with feelings and desires – nobody can argue with feelings. But, a rational person can rationalize things outside their best interests. If all you care about is money, then them offering your current salary plus $1,000 makes you better off, so take this dog-shit deal, Mr. Rational. But a person who feels this will be insulted. It is not in the best interests of prospective employers to insult you, but they will fight for the best deal for them that they can convince you to take. This is less likely if you've developed and communicated a strong narrative for your search.

Dave Chappelle's *Chappelle's Show* was an extremely successful sketch comedy from the early 2000s, responsible for many of the catchphrases you may still hear from millennials. "Yeeaaah!" or "I'm Rick James, bitch" are most people's favorites. However, I was always a fan of Samuel Jackson Beer – "How's it taste, Mo****fu****!?" Audiences revered the show, and Chappelle was making the most money he'd ever made. However, he felt he got a bad deal, so he surprisingly walked away mid-season from a multimillion- dollar contract. Comedy Central owned the rights to do with the show whatever they wanted.

In his 2020 special *Unforgiven*, Chappelle talks about his struggles working with the network and them sidelining him in meetings before walking away because he signed over control to them. Years later, and shortly after receiving the streaming rights, Netflix took down *Chappelle's Show* from its service

Ch. 11 The Working Class Works Too Hard 153

because streaming it upset Dave. Dave didn't lawyer up; he didn't call the executives to demand Netflix take it down or give them a million rational arguments for why they need to remove the content. He simply told the Netflix executives that streaming the show made him feel bad. He is a human, expecting to be treated as such. Starting the conversation on that note led to a lucrative comedy special deal with Netflix that wouldn't have happened if he was more aggressive.

Many business books refute my assertion on anti-rationality. They want you to be uber-rational and support yourself with data. I'm a finance-educated banker; I understand numbers and data – hell, I even had a chapter on data – and advice to be rational is horse-shit. The Bureau of Labor Statistics (BLS) data is an excellent tool for understanding what to expect. However, if you inform the employer that the BLS says a job should pay $60,000, they'll tell you it only pays $45,000 because the descriptions don't align 100%, or they'll find another reason to support their stance. If they've decided to make you a bad deal, then you've failed in the first step of the negotiation – building the right narrative. Walk away. If you press them for more and they flip-flop only to offer you substantially more, you'll just be offended they played games. Perhaps they offer you a promise of a salary bump in a few months. You'll be very disappointed when they later renege on their deal. Walk away and try elsewhere. There will be another opportunity.

I was waiting for the bus one evening and saw a bum talking to another rider who was obviously a corporate drone. The drone rationalized to the bum why he couldn't give him money. Unfazed, the bum countered all points, and they argued for 5 minutes or so. The bum cuckolded the man into handing over his money.

Next, the bum saunters my way.

Bum: "Can you spare a few dollars?"

Me: "No."

Bum: "No? That's all?"

He stepped back, wide-eyed and surprised I didn't provide an excuse.

He expected me to give him an excuse so he could refute it and try to convince me he deserved my money more than me. He knows corporate drones are rational people, and he feeds on our rationality day in day out. He didn't even look like a bum and probably wasn't even one. He was just a guy looking for a sucker. Rationality is for suckers, and there's a saying: never give a sucker an even break.

You can't refute just a no. Same goes for a job. "I want $60,000." That's it. What will they say, "You don't deserve that"? If your expectations are wild, perhaps they will. But, if you do your research and request a fair amount, then anything less is an insult. If you give reasons why, you're providing the other side an opportunity to say why not. A rational person can be convinced, and managers have far more experience persuading people than you do.

My wife's residency program is with an organization that does not sway. Her team has tried and failed time after time to discuss issues with management. Management never says no; they just always consider the team's solutions and never provide tangible changes. My wife and another resident wanted to raise concerns about the new schedule requiring them to work late every Friday. They're supposed to have protected time that day per the program guidance, and plus, it's just plain bullshit. Friday didn't need to be the day they worked late; it was arbitrary and certainly felt to them that the program did it just because they had the power to get away with it. She and her colleague drafted a well-written professional request for a meeting and outlined all of their points. They avoided subjective reasonings (such as "it's right before the weekend, screw you") and made a logical argument. The pair sent their well-written argument, and the manager replied, refuting all items presented. Their requested meeting was declined, and they worked late on Fridays for 12 months. Never underestimate a lousy manager.

Also, your coworkers lie. Most people inflate their salary when asked by peers how much they make. Nobody wants to be the chump. Don't feel bad when your salary doesn't match up.

As a closing thought, there are bad companies, bad positions, bad managers, bad everything – there are also good companies and people, but that's another topic. Know what you're working with and find the right fit. A company that doesn't reward hard work isn't going to start rewarding hard work because you show up, work hard, and have negotiation experience. Likewise, they have a budget for each role, and no matter how productive you are, they will pay you within their pre-set range. These are external constraints to your career that you can only mitigate by changing roles, companies, or industries.

Pro-tip: If someone tells you Pareto's Principle isn't true, they are using corporate speak to say, "I am a useless 80%'r."

Chapter Exercise: Best Qualities

List your three best qualities/traits and note if they are quantitative or qualitative.

1.

2.

3.

Chapter Exercise: Comparison

Compare your qualities to the job posting exercise in Chapter 7.

Do they match? (Y / N)

Chapter 12:

The Working Class Must Work Harder.

I told you I would contradict myself, and here it is. There is a balance between putting in the required effort and not too much effort. Unfortunately, employers have their thumb on the scale.

More than likely, if you have no connections to the company, are working for bad managers, and lack enough experience to leave, you will be the 20%'r doing 80% of the work. It sucks, but it's the reality.

I was a 30-year-old veteran with strong military performance, early promotions, management experience, and two bachelor's degrees, starting my first entry-level professional position for $54,000 per year as a credit analyst in commercial banking. Most people starting in this role are 22 with no experience except an eight-week internship. Presumably, they made the same salary as me, but they may have made more. Before I graduated, I applied for over 50

Ch. 12 The Working Class Must Work Harder

jobs, contacted dozens of bankers and recruiters, and had to lower my salary expectations to get this job. This was 2016.

More recently, I have seen entry-level commercial banking analyst positions starting at over $75,000 per year, a salary not available to me at the time despite my background. I had many interviews and offers, and although the position I accepted was not the highest paying, none offered me over $60,000. My offers were roughly aligned with my expectations for someone with zero experience. Should I have bitched and complained and not taken the position to stand for fairness based on my other unrelated experience? Perhaps, but there wasn't much variance in the salaries, so I was probably getting roughly a fair deal. Conceivably the perceived higher risk of a 30-year-old with an unconventional background offset my greater experience (here's me rationalizing like a *sucker*). No matter how wrong people's biases are, they are a constraint.

I would not be where I am today if I blindly thought I deserved more and fought for it. I also would not be where I am if my riskiness were actually as high as they perceived it. I'm an Examiner in Corporate and Investment Banking's Specialty Finance Group at the 5th largest bank in the world (2nd largest if you exclude the state-run Chinese banks). Only a handful of people do what I do. Few others with my experience level, even with connections, are doing as well as I am today, seven years later.

Have I worked harder than others? Yes.

Did I take the time outside of work to learn industry best practices? Yes.

Did I wait for my employer to tell me what was important or what they wanted? Sometimes, but generally not.

Ch. 12 The Working Class Must Work Harder

Is this to toot my own horn? No. This is to tell you it is OK to work harder. To live is to work – there is no getting around it. I worked very hard and much harder than most of my banking peers, but it was the only way to progress. If you're working hard and underpaid, discover why they're not paying you more and change what you can control. In the previous chapter, I said there is a limit to how much jobs pay. Take a stand when you're underpaid in their range, but finding a new job (i.e., a better fit) may be the only solution.

Many companies will give you a chance if you are willing to work very hard. These are mostly poorly run companies that do borderline sketchy business, but they will give you a chance (probably because professionals in the industry will not work for them). If you can't find an opportunity at the major players, apply your way down the list. The more prestigious the company, the harder it will be for an outsider to break into a great role – they receive too many job applications, reducing the likelihood yours ever gets reviewed.

Don't get caught in the trap of taking a dogshit role at a great institution. I see very few people actually work themselves up from this scenario – don't think you'll be one of the few to break through without strong connections. You are not the only factor, and corporations are not meritocracies. It is probably better to work for a smaller, less prestigious company and gain great experience that you can use to apply for a better role at that larger organization later if you still want it.

Anyway, a few years at one of these companies that will give anyone a shot, supplemented with external training and learning, will do wonders for your career. However, beware. They provide a lot of people a chance. This means a lot of people who don't pull their weight (i.e., 80%'rs may be more like

90%'rs...). They will expect you to pick up the slack when required – which is always. Managers use manipulative tactics to convince you to do even more for less and make you feel like you are too incompetent to leave. You may have heard of *gaslighting*: the purposeful manipulation of facts and a psychological game to make you feel insecure or anxious. These companies use gas lighting extensively, but my wife tells me I'm just paranoid.

To avoid being gas-lit, separate yourself from your work and set a standard for your deliverables. You turn in your monthly report, and your manager wants to revise the dates for only the first through the fifteenth; give them those dates without any feelings. You return it, and now the manager wants the dates to be the original first through the thirtieth; give them that without any feelings even though it took you extra effort. Set an expectation that revisions will slow down your other projects. Setting expectations this way is called *managing up*. They will hate this and load you with unbearable levels of work to keep you producing while under their thumb. Despite often being arbitrary, they will try to make you feel responsible for their revisions. Don't work harder because they can't make a decision. This is incredibly hard to overcome unless you already do not give a shit. If you give a shit, remember that they are not going to fire you for moderately reducing your already solid productivity.

The good news is that being good and working hard makes you valuable in tough times. Very few 20%'rs will be laid off in a recession.

Progressing in your career is an uphill battle; too many people want a high-paying job. Some people are good at their jobs. Some people know the boss. Unless you know the boss,

Ch. 12 The Working Class Must Work Harder

you can only do one thing to increase your chances; put in the effort.

If you wonder why you can't just be the 80%'r doing less, it's because you are not that person. You wouldn't be reading this if you were because you'd probably be thrilled about your position. Also, I cannot advise how to achieve the 80%'r status. My life has involved hard work and over-contribution in every role I've ever had. I imagine 80%'rs come partly from incompetence, nepotism, and laziness. Does that sound like you?

George Costanza of *Seinfeld* is an 80%'r. Probably more like a 0%'r. He does nothing to bring value to his employers. Never had done anything. He sits in his office and acts stressed out, so his managers think they're working him too hard. He jumps from job to job, relies on luck to obtain what he wants, and cuts corners everywhere he can – most critically, the cheap envelopes that kill his fiancé, Susan. George does not take control of his own life. He is consistently manipulated by Kramer into hair-brained schemes that never work out well for anyone. He's moving but never getting anywhere because he always wants a good deal. Costanza is no Ted Danson.

I do not know how to be a Costanza, but I know planning and hard work (aligned with values) helped me, and it is entirely replicable. Winning the lottery is not.

Pro-tip: Go apply with the New York Yankees if you think Costanza-isms will help you acquire what you want. Or skip the effort and just buy a lottery ticket.

Ch. 12 The Working Class Must Work Harder
Chapter Exercise: Managing

Imagine you are your current manager. List the three most critical quantitative skills for your employees and rate your actual performance in each.

1.

Performance: Weak / Average / Strong

2.

Performance: Weak / Average / Strong

3.

Performance: Weak / Average / Strong

How are you determining your rating?

Are you rating fairly (neither too harsh nor too soft)?

Using your peers as the baseline, are you doing too much or too little?

Chapter 13:

Being Good may Mean Sucking at Your Job

Earlier, we discussed how organizations may value poor quality if it helps them meet their goals because good is all about perspective. In business, meeting the defined goal is the objective; regardless of your personal feelings or beliefs. When I moved to Arizona with my former employer, I took over a commercial loan portfolio filled with dogshit problem loans. All the former bankers on those loans had left the company, and I could not corroborate the details provided in their reports. Many loans were originated for start-ups using projected performance that never materialized for the borrowers.

For the deals in this portfolio, little worked as the underwriter expected. Talking to the borrowers, the underwriter also misrepresented much of what was documented about their operations. Was this lousy underwriting? It depends on who you ask.

Ch. 13 Being Good May Mean Sucking At Your Job

Underwriting: Accepting risk for payment. In commercial lending, underwriters analyze a company's comprehensive risk to repaying the loan and structure the deal based on the key risks. This includes analyzing the company's financial performance (historical and projected financial statement analysis), operations (including their customers and suppliers), senior management and owners, industry, and any other relevant facts material to the question of repayment.

Some of these loans were delinquent, and as my manager put it regarding one borrower, "We believe this company is a money-laundering operation." That company paid over a million dollars a year in interest to us.

So, were the former bankers bad at their jobs? They had extreme sales goals and were incredibly understaffed. What should they have done, not met their goals to perform lengthy due diligence? They gave the organization exactly what it asked for. The bank wouldn't have appreciated an extended underwriting period, and not meeting their goals in order to provide higher quality would be considered poor performance.

This group was the shining star of the bank while they were producing such dogshit regularly. Before transferring, my prior group was hassled about this team's incredible productivity and repeatedly questioned why we couldn't perform like them. The "money-laundering operation?" Leadership highlighted them at our annual all-employee extravaganza as a "tough deal" this group was able to cross over the finish line and proceeded to motivate us to do more deals just like it. The bank loved this team. If there was an employee who couldn't get shit deals funded, they wouldn't have lasted, not with this culture. Only when the market president on down the line left the bank did everything come crashing down. Nobody who remained was

Ch. 13 Being Good May Mean Sucking At Your Job   165

familiar enough with these companies nor incentivized to lie. And there was a lot of shit. These bankers made big bonuses and were highly compensated for their actions. I didn't earn nearly the same compensation or respect as I cleaned up their mess. Additionally, they didn't always operate this way as the worst deals were primarily originated in the prior three years – implying something had recently changed the culture and risk appetite.

I stated earlier there are two ways to grow: (i) a growing industry or (ii) stealing market share from competitors. Technically, there is a third – developing a new market. What's the easiest way to grow a market? Take excessive risk. Many of those terrible loans were to companies or serial entrepreneurs who had been around for years and never received a formal bank loan before – they were previously unbankable until we looked at them. The companies would have loved to borrow, and I'm sure they tried elsewhere. Our advantage was getting loans approved that shouldn't have been done. The bankers prospected the lowest-hanging fruit.

Who sucks at their job? The underwriter who misrepresented the facts and outright lied to obtain approval, made a boatload of money for himself and the bank, and left before everything blew up (and subsequently received a new high-paying job at another bank and presumably does the same thing there)? Or the guy who elevates the risks and tries to manage them appropriately? One guy made the bank a lot of money for a couple of years; the other lost the bank a lot of money as he downgraded customers, called them in default, or booted them from the bank (I would argue that I saved the bank millions in losses in the medium-term, but that is much less apparent than the immediately visible profits from poor practices). In this case, 10 or so guys made the bank a lot of money. It wouldn't have happened if it wasn't condoned. It should have been evident that they were taking on excessive risk given the growth rates. I had to repeatedly explain why they were wrong without a thank you for catching the risks, along with a lot of active discouragement. If my concerns were overstated, they could have told me the risks were acceptable. But they weren't.

A suspected money laundering operation is unacceptable (our compliance department uncovered this risk before I was assigned). In another instance, one banker served on the board of directors of one of his borrowers. The file noted a risk manager raised the concern of conflict of interest, but the market president shut down the fears and conversation. My review of the deal found that the same banker released the bank's lien on collateral without oversight or record, and another lender scooped up first position (meaning we may not have collateral on the loan). Worse yet, the year I was assigned the account, the borrower's auditor raised substantial doubt about the borrower's ability to continue operations (meaning the auditor believed the borrower could be out of business within a year's time). Now, we have no collateral on a borrower headed toward bankruptcy. When I elevated these concerns to correct the issue, do you think it was praised and corrected? Absolutely not. Despite having our legal counsel's confirmation, the approver directly questioned my judgment and blamed me for the lien release (which made no sense as it happened years before I joined the bank and with me clearly identifying the responsible banker). Did facts matter? No. The bank actively discouraged troublemakers like me, who cost them revenue and stock price growth. They wanted to ignore

Ch. 13 Being Good May Mean Sucking At Your Job

problems to the very end until after the borrower is in bankruptcy – keeping the bonuses flowing for as long as possible. That job sucked, and I left shortly after that event. But this was a valuable experience.

You can take this story to mean one of two things. First, just give your organization what they want, don't make trouble, and don't care more than the company's leaders – they will make your life miserable if you don't meld with the culture. Or, screw 'em. There are standards and ethics, and that job sucked. By not listening to bad managers and by studying industry best practices externally, I learned enough to earn my next role at a world-class institution, allowing me to start contributing immediately and providing the flexibility to raise my family. I also have an insane conflict tolerance now. Further illustrating the ethics of that company, coworkers were reportedly discouraged from taking their maternity/paternity benefits, while I enjoyed 10 weeks of paid time off without hassle from my new boss. So, there's also that...

I know I sound bitter, but there is no correct answer here.

Doing what is *right* in the perspective of this organization meant making up information about borrowers to obtain loan approval. *Right* in the context of the banking industry meant learning industry best practices and setting a standard for myself. I was not rewarded immediately at the organizational level, but I was rewarded later by finding a higher-paying, more balanced role that appreciates my contribution. That would not have occurred if I had fit into the first bank's culture; my new manager would have laughed me out of the interview for being such a jabroni. Understanding the right decision will take years to develop, and this book is intended to help create that framework. But *right* is often very ambiguous, and it becomes even more so when many interests are involved. Well-paid positions require dealing with more ambiguity, uncertainty, and competing interests.

I cannot tell you what the right thing is; however, never do the wrong thing.

The wrong decision is much easier to understand than the right decision. The definite wrong thing is that which hurts someone else to your benefit or fails to help someone for your benefit. Take this statement at face value, and don't overthink it. This is a gut instinct kind of problem – like, should we bank a suspected money launderer to meet our goals? Undoubtedly, no.

Another example is my resident physician friend seeking to make a million dollars a year. Unbearable levels of work were piled onto the residents, and morale within the group was severely stressed. Something needed to be done, so I implored her and others (including my wife) to take a stand and just decline changes to the schedule. This resident refused to say no to anything asked of her precisely because she wanted a job at that hospital after graduation. She reported the organization promised her a fellowship in the field that pays a million dollars a year and a job upon graduation, and she refused to jeopardize that opportunity. She was unwilling to take a stand and then actively discouraged others from taking action so as to not rock the boat and compromise her expected earnings.

That resident stood with the organization when she knew it was wrong, and they bailed on her. She was not selected for the fellowship and will almost certainly never make her anticipated million-dollar salary, despite it appearing to be a sure thing just a few months earlier.

I was the top banker at my credit union branch years ago. I handled more transactions, originated more loans, and cross-sold more products, by far, than anyone else. I confirmed this by reviewing the work of bankers in my branch and a few other branches. I never sold a product to someone who wouldn't benefit, either. My manager tried discouraging me from leaving this job to go back to school for finance, stating, "It's not going to change anything" for me. She even said that to customers about me leaving. As if retail banking was the pinnacle of success. She worked in the organization's interests to keep her golden goose from vanishing. She didn't care about me personally or for my long-term personal growth.

This *leader* valued the short-term benefit for the organization by keeping me. Managers indeed have an obligation to do what's right for the organization, but was convincing me I was making a mistake by returning to school the correct tactic? No. She often did the wrong thing; you can bet I let Human Resources have it in my exit interview. She probably told everyone I didn't care about them after I left.

That manager had a long-term career goal of becoming a regional manager of several branches. Now, at the time of this writing, more than seven years later, she is not a regional manager, nor even a branch manager any longer. Instead, she is an accounting specialist (i.e., an accountant's assistant) at a small business, certainly making less than she did as a branch manager. Her husband is in the same role he was in before, so it doesn't appear they're doing so well she was able to step down by choice. This is not about the money. The fact is, she did the wrong thing over and over again and was rewarded with a demotion, almost certain never to meet her goals. Her manager was equally malicious in her role as regional manager (they were a *good* team together). She was also demoted and no longer manages people. Neither looked out for their employees, repeatedly did the wrong things, and thus jeopardized the achievement of their long-term goals. Both individuals lasted only about three years in their positions of power.

Long-term success depends on working hard and doing the right thing, always. Or at least not doing the wrong thing.

If you're thinking, "But what if it benefits me at the moment?" think again. Ignoring the obvious ethical question, do you really want to risk knowing you did the wrong thing for personal benefit and then never even benefit from it – you do the wrong thing for nothing or just a pittance? What are you willing to sell your soul for? I hope it's enough.

My former sales manager in commercial banking liked to ask prospective borrowers about their offers from other banks. He would even ask to see their term sheets from different banks before providing his. He didn't want them to show us. He only respected the companies who declined to reveal the other terms. He did this to see how well he could trust them and how much he could screw the ones who showed him. Anyone who provided a term sheet was deemed untrustworthy, and nobody feels sympathy for the dishonest guy who gets screwed. He probably did this to employment applicants as well.

A prospective employer asked for an actual sample of my underwriting. The interviewer wanted me to send him a deal I originated so he could "see my writing skills." This would involve me sending sensitive information to my personal account and sharing it with a competitor, and it was an absolute trap. Would I have gotten the job? Probably, but they never would have trusted me, and my career would be at a dead-end. I declined and killed the conversation. You'll always be a

Ch. 13 Being Good May Mean Sucking At Your Job

liability if you show you're willing to do the wrong thing.

The film *Amsterdam* provides a great example of values and doing the right thing. *Amsterdam* is a wonderful film starring Christian Bale, John David Washington, and Margot Robbie (whom I call the Trio), set in the 1930s prior to World War II. The Trio investigates the death of the male leads' former World War I commanding officer, General Bill Meekins. They enlist the help of another General, Gil Dillenbeck, played by Robert DeNiro, to determine the reason for Meekins' suspected murder.

The Trio acts on a very micro level. They don't have the full scope of the details, but the death of their beloved General doesn't sit well with them. They know something is wrong despite limited to no evidence and are driven to action. They are looking to do the right thing. Only when General Dillenbeck becomes involved does the conspiracy begin to present itself – he is a person of great importance and a favored populist leader among the nation's veterans. The conspirators work to recruit him with enticing payments for helping their cause but provide limited details on what he is helping them with or what their organization values. At the climax, we learn their objective is to overthrow the U.S.'s democratic government to instate a dictatorship like those developing in Europe at the time. The conspirators are prominent fictional CEOs of companies made up for the movie: Nevins Telecommunications, Belport Chemicals International, and Jeffers Publishing, along with the fictional philanthropist Tom Voze and his wife.

After revealing their plot to the General, the Vozes urge the General to do the *right* thing. The *right* thing involves ignoring the murder of his friend, General Meekins, and encouraging the nation's veterans to overthrow the government. They provide the speech he is to give.

Ms. Voze states, "If you improvise and get lost in the woods of some complicated criminal situation over Meekins' death, it will reflect badly on you."

The couple demands that General Dillenbeck take money for a foundation that doesn't exist, advises they could do so much more for him, and warns him if he wanders from the path they have set.

Mr. Voze chillingly goes on to say: "Someone, not me. They will take your face, your name, put it in the New York Times, and wipe their dog's ass with it. Think of everything you've accomplished in your life – it will be forgotten, erased. You'll be treated like an old kook and buried by history. That's what they can do. Make the right speech."

"Don't make the mistake like Bill Meekins," Ms. Voze then adds, admitting to the murder.

The General stands up for what is genuinely the right thing. He informs the public of the recruitment efforts to overthrow the government, and the conspirators are arrested. An assassination attempt is made on his life, but the Trio's efforts stop it. Perhaps never taking any action against the conspirators could have been the right thing given the lack of evidence, but no conspiracy then would have ever been uncovered. The General indeed does the right thing by exposing the conspiracy, despite all of the pros and cons suggesting the opposite, not just because of the lack of initial evidence but given the extensive reach of the conspirators. Notably, the conspirators encouraged him to do the *right* thing from their perspective.

The purpose here is not just to show the right thing but also to question why this film was released in 2022 and why the

Ch. 13 Being Good May Mean Sucking At Your Job

writer selected key details. The writer made up fictional companies as conspirators but named the New York Times specifically as the General is blackmailed. The fictional Jeffers Publishing is a media outlet that could have served the same purpose. Still, they explicitly named the New York Times when they proclaimed the conspiracy's reach and threatened to slander the General's name into oblivion. The Trio had no explicit evidence of a conspiracy or malicious plot to kill General Meekins. They acted on a hunch because the facts didn't align, and that hunch turned out to be correct.

Obviously, this is a fictional story, and just because the writer implies something, it doesn't mean it's true about the New York Times, large international companies, or American politics. But current events may explain why a movie with a star-studded cast about characters doing the right thing is made after the contested 2020 election. They act on just a hunch with no evidence and get caught up in a conspiracy involving high-powered interests and collusion with the media to overthrow a democratically elected government. Further, the explicit naming and threats by the conspirators regarding the name-brand New York Times exemplify the modern news media and social media's reliance on and collusion toward a dominant narrative with the help of the authorities.

Remember the fact-checkers during Donald Trump's presidency – There is no evidence to suggest the Hunter Biden laptop story is true, or worse yet, 51 leading intelligence experts report the Hunter Biden laptop story is Russian disinformation and the subsequent social-media censorship before the presidential election. The same thing happened with COVID and the 2016 and 2020 election claims, which have since turned out differently than first presented. We now know the FBI acted in bad faith by opening the Trump-Russia investigation, the CIA helped the Biden 2020 campaign defend against the Biden laptop story (despite it being authentic), more and more government agencies report the likelihood of COVID's lab origins, the potentially harmful side-effects of the COVID vaccine on the young, and that unconstitutional changes and questionable practices were implemented for the 2020 election in critical geographies. Worse yet, corrupted media displayed no such discretion nor fear of misinformation as they ran Trump- Russia collusion stories regularly.

The Department of Justice has now found that the FBI opened their investigation without any real evidence and was likely politically motivated against Trump. The investigators weren't working on a hunch about Trump-Russia collusion because facts didn't align; they regularly disregarded evidence contrary to their narrative, disregarded standard practice, disregarded intelligence agency expertise, illegally altered CIA communication to obtain intrusive warrants, had no corroborating evidence that Trump or anyone on his campaign had been in contact with Russia, and relied on "speculation and rumor" from a suspected Russian spy to whom they provided immunity and even compensated for the information. Yes, the FBI provided immunity and paid a suspected Russian spy (their words, not mine) for rumors about President Trump to support their unwarranted investigation. Perhaps the blackmail scene in Amsterdam reflects the equally poor treatment and defamation of the once-favored *America's Mayor*, Rudy Giuliani, as he stood with Trump on election claims.

But federal investigators have disproven election claims by not finding substantial evidence of fraud, right? Sorry, that's not how it works.

Ch. 13 Being Good May Mean Sucking At Your Job

Harry Markopolos discovered Bernie Madoff's $65 billion Ponzi scheme years before the U.S. Securities and Exchange Commission. He figured it out fairly easily. See, Mr. Markopolos found that the reported derivative investments in Bernie Madoff's fund were greater than the number in existence, and no one on the Chicago Board Options Exchange (where one would invest in such items) ever made a trade with Mr. Madoff – therefore, fraud. Duh...While Mr. Madoff "invested" in more options derivatives than were even in existence, we can view the situation as conceptually similar to investing in stocks for our purposes here. Simplified: if a fund reports that it holds 100 billion shares of Apple stock, but there are only 16 billion shares outstanding, even a total jabroni would realize they're lying by using common sense. But he had even more evidence based on statistics.

Mr. Markopolos repeatedly provided evidence to the SEC, and they refused to investigate for several years. Finally, in early 2006, the SEC opened a case file into Madoff, and I'm sure Markopolos was relieved. Oh, wait, nope – the SEC closed the case 11 months later without a full investigation due to "no evidence of fraud" (and that is a direct quote from the SEC; sound familiar?).

How did Bernie Madoff end up in jail? He turned himself in.

Common sense can be much more enlightening than a narrative created by a supposed authority. Just like the investments of earlier chapters, narratives are developed to get you to feel good about doing what you know in your heart doesn't make sense. Your manager will create a narrative to get you to do more and even the wrong things. The wrong things could be just poor practices that keep you from developing (so

Ch. 13 Being Good May Mean Sucking At Your Job

you cannot leave for a better position), or it may be more sinister, like keeping the Ponzi scheme going. Decide what you are willing to do and what your soul is worth beforehand.

Ch. 13 Being Good May Mean Sucking At Your Job

Chapter Exercise: The Right Thing

Detail a tough decision you needed to make. Note whether you stand by your decision today and if other stakeholders feel the same. For example, if it involved your spouse, did/do they concur with your decision?

1.

Do you stand by your decision today: (Y / N)

Do stakeholders agree: (Y / N)

Were you rewarded over the long-run: (Y / N)

Chapter 14:

Don't Care More than Your Manager

Alright, I'm doing it again. Did I make the right choice at that bank by elevating risks in the portfolio of bad loans? I don't know. I am now better off after practicing prudent risk management, but it was an excruciating many years with that company. Would I be as developed without that experience – absolutely not. But I could have been equally undeveloped in that role with a different tenacity to learn. And there was a *good enough* standard for the position I was certainly exceeding and wouldn't have been penalized for if I maintained it. I was miserable doing the right thing and questioned my sanity at times. Harry Markopolos feared for his life after exposing Bernie Madoff. Do not follow our examples blindly.

My problem is that I cannot do the wrong thing or unsee a problem once I uncover it – I elevate issues and risks that I find (I cannot fix them without involving other parties). Managers tend to hate that. They're forced to take action once there is documentation about a problem. They're not going to ignore

Ch. 14 Don't Care More Than Your Manager 179

it. What they don't want is for you or me to elevate it. They want us (workers) to be unethical because that gets business done, sales goals met, and bonuses for everyone. And if it blows up, they blame the workers for not raising the issue, and they keep their jobs. A bit of ignorance goes a long way.

In Malcolm Gladwell's 2019 best-seller *Talking to Strangers*, he recounts actual events of the U.S. intelligence community's problem with Cuban double agents. These actors infiltrated the CIA and other U.S. intelligence agencies by providing key "intel" (narratives created by Fidel Castro et al. to shape the U.S.'s understanding of Cuba). But the U.S. had a plan to handle double-agent risk – polygraph tests for agents in the field. No, this is not about the faults of lie detectors. In fact, the tests were too accurate as many of the double agents repeatedly failed. What was management's solution? Ignore the results and reem out the administrators of the tests – they clearly suck at their job with so many failures. However, operatives failed for very good reasons – they were Cuban spies.

No, this isn't the private sector. But it is an important lesson regarding the *agency problem* – managers were not incentivized to think of what's best for national security (use the results of the failed lie detector tests to boot the double agents out the door.), and so they didn't. We want to think our national security directors care about our country more than anything else, but they don't. It wouldn't look good to their bosses if their operatives were Cuban spies. Instead, they covered their own asses because that is a manager's number one job.

If you're good (objectively good, not subjectively good, as discussed earlier), you will find issues and need to do something. If you're just good enough, you don't find as many problems because your due diligence is relatively weak. A happy medium is fitting your quality to your manager's expectations. I was given a boatload of work and blamed after inheriting bad loans, implying my boss wanted the bare minimum from me, or in other words, to stop raising issues. Unfortunately, I am apparently a sucker or a masochist and objectively good at my job, and I just find issues. I intend that if it is immaterial, my boss can make that judgment. It never was immaterial because I have a solid understanding of what matters – it's why I have progressed rapidly. However, this led to very unpleasant working conditions for me. Still, I understand the risks I am taking against my happiness when I elevate concerns. Beware of the risks you face if your company has a similar culture.

Caring more than your manager creates multiple problems:
1) They think you're trying to steal their job, and
2) You're creating problems they have to solve (more work for them). Bad managers will force you to solve such problems but give you ambiguous advice, steamroll meetings, create burdensome busy work, and additional analysis, all meant to tell you it's time to shut the f*** up. Listen carefully if you value happiness in the immediate term.

Fit the culture, don't raise a stink, keep your head down, and do what your boss says the way they like it done. You're a burden on your manager with anything more or less.

Pro-Tip: Scrap this entire chapter and everything just discussed here. The trick is to find a manager or organization that *fits* you.

Ch. 14 Don't Care More Than Your Manager   181

Chapter Exercise: Fit-ness

Name a job or relationship you were unhappy in.

1.

Are you still in it? (Y / N)

Chapter Exercise: Fit-ness v.2

Name a job or relationship you were happy in.

1.

Are you still in it? (Y / N)

Chapter Exercise: Compare

Detail three reasons why you were happy or unhappy in these situations.

1.

2.

3.

Chapter 15:

Nepotism

Nepotism is alive and well in large organizations. Within the context of Pareto's Principle and good enough, nepotism is rational for managers to practice.

Nepotism: Providing advantages to family or friends due to relationships, not skill or experience.

This is not to say nepotism is good or efficient, but it makes sense why it exists. First off, if 80% of your employees only contribute 20% of the output, what is just another unproductive cog in the wheel out of thousands? Nepotism allows managers to deepen their relationship with stakeholders, and the large organization will barely notice the lack of productivity. The opportunity advantages the new employee, so they will look out for their best interest by taking the job. Like my underqualified banking colleague, it is doubtful her lack of skills will impact her performance reviews as expectations of her will be reduced. The hiring manager knows she's not qualified; that's why they went outside of the normal process and straight to top management in the first place. This could also relate to the organization's expectation of good enough.

Good enough allows a worker to perform at a lower level than their pay grade expects or provides an out for lower performance based on some qualitative characteristic that helps rationalize away the weakness – e.g., they're a weak analyst but a strong *leader*.

Beyond these factors, there is, unfortunately, a legitimate reason why many professionals' children have more advantages – my daughter will learn the lessons from my mistakes, which I pass down to her. Additionally, she will benefit from a career in banking or medicine due to her parent's experience and perspective. For instance, I can teach her all about finance, banking, Microsoft Excel, financial analysis, accounting, and more – things I never started learning until I was 30. Nobody showed me the way, and my parents didn't know the first thing about finance or accounting. If you're reading this, I also doubt your parents taught you those skills. She will get that early on.

My parents encouraged the oldest children to go to college so that we would not struggle as they did, but they didn't know what made college meaningful and provided little guidance on what degrees to pursue. They then actively discouraged my much younger brother from pursuing an accounting degree due to the older children's college failures (obtaining useless degrees with no focus on skills and incurring burdensome levels of debt in the process), not understanding there is a crucial difference between an accounting and arts degree. They did not research programs, nor did they know accounting graduates have nearly 100% job placement, are in extremely high demand, and starting salaries are almost as much as my parents ever made at their peak – the debt will be of minimal concern. My younger brother would have access to me, which could supplement his education experience. My parents didn't know this because they were high school dropouts lacking basic research skills necessary to inquire about career prospects. They still did a pretty good job, considering they had their first child at 20 years old, but their perspective was narrow. This is how most working-class parents operate.

Alternatively, my forever wife's dad knew what she was going to do starting at a very early age, despite himself never appreciating the same level of success he bestowed upon her. Her family is very middle class. Her dad worked for the U.S. Postal Service, and her mom was a nurse working part-time for much of my wife's upbringing. However, her dad researched the U.S. Naval Academy, how to apply, what they value in an applicant, and built her childhood experiences around the goal of her attending. He was very involved, and that is an advantage. My parent's guidance of "go to college so you don't struggle like me" was about the extent of their involvement. They wouldn't even release their tax returns to help my siblings and me apply for financial aid (which we would have qualified for and reduced the debt burden they eventually became so worried about for my youngest brother). They didn't understand what was important, why college, or what classes mattered. They just thought college mattered, and never going was why they struggled. Four of five children got arts degrees and never did anything with them. Despite higher education, three kids are still working class and no better off than their parents. I now have an advantage by recognizing these failures;

Ch. 15 Nepotism 185

my children will have the same. You can also benefit from the lessons here. The ones who don't learn this lesson are doomed to repeat their parents' mistakes.

My children will have tangible advantages, or *privileges* as we like to say these days, which I never had. But privilege is a range, not an absolute. President Obama's daughters will have opportunities neither I nor my children will ever have. Not just because people will want to do favors for the former President's children, but the Obamas know something about the world I do not – love him or hate him, something got him into the Presidency, which he will certainly pass on to his children. I don't know what that something is, nor do I have his connections, and therefore, my children will not benefit from Obama's juice. Hunter Biden's dad was a Senator, Vice President, and President. Despite his failures, he is still financially successful, and out of prison, given his dad's connections. His dad handled Ukraine and China as VP. From where did Hunter obtain investment and opportunity? Ukraine and China. He is wealthy by any objective measure (unless he's blown it all on hookers and coke) because of his dad. In contrast, my children will not be wealthy, but they will know how banking or medicine works, which is their pre- paid ticket to the upper-middle class if they want it.

Despite my parents' shortcomings, they still encouraged us to do more, and they cared – that is an advantage. I may not have developed the desire to progress if they never inspired more (despite sometimes encouraging the wrong things). Many parents do not promote growth, nor do they care. That may describe your life, but you are an adult. It's time to acknowledge this failure and move on. Don't get stuck in the past or on who has what privilege you do not. But that's easier said than done because you are still at a disadvantage when you compare yourself to others.

My siblings are stuck and discouraged by the lack of privilege bestowed by my parents. I know many others in the same position. They cannot move forward, while I never gave two shits about what privileges my parents did not provide, and I just kept moving. This is a facts and values differential: we know our parents' limitations, but my siblings would instead make excuses and place blame instead of taking the reins over their lives. In business school, we call this concept *locus of control*, and studies show that an internal locus of control (the belief that individual actions matter) is required to achieve your goals, regardless of reality. This doesn't mean you will automatically become successful with this mindset, but it is a prerequisite. Without an internal locus of control, you are doomed to a life of the lottery. Take it in because this is the only time I will tell you mindset actually matters – Life hacks!

A former manager had over twenty years of experience in banking, was the son of a retired banker, and made a few hundred thousand dollars a year, if not more. With all the privilege in the world doing what Daddy did, he was not a great banker. Not only was he a terrible people manager (coworkers' words, not mine), but he couldn't make decisions, had a tenuous grasp on banking in general, and I absolutely believe he did not know what he was doing most of the time (okay, they were also my words). This was the company that valued incompetent risk managers, mind you.

His buddy was also our market president. They worked together at their last job, and when the market president was hired at this company to lead the sales function (which was deserved), he brought over his buddy to manage risk (which was not deserved). Relationships matter, and they count more than anything in the private sector. You can be completely incompetent and hold executive-level roles provided by associations, or be 100% competent and struggle to find something entry-level.

One would hope the perspective gained from being a second-generation banker would improve his performance, but it didn't. We butted heads on many items because he didn't know how to structure loans, wanted every borrower to fit inside a narrow box, and refused to listen to the advice of our internal experts when they advised. When I interviewed for other roles outside of that organization, I provided a lending scenario and asked the interviewer how they would structure the deal – never once did any of the managers structure the loan the way my old boss did. These hiring managers often stared at me wide-eyed and proclaimed they would not even touch such a dog-shit deal. This is how I knew I could work for someone. At my new company, I described how my old manager would structure loans to the head of our group. I gave him the facts unemotionally, with no indication I approved or did not approve of those methods, and he promptly called my former manager a "fucking idiot." This guy reports to our company's board of directors – he's no jabroni.

Conservatives tend to espouse meritocratic values. Most believe people should receive a fair deal. Conservatives tend to disagree with diversity initiatives, not because they are racists or think minorities or women deserve less; they just believe you get what you put in and shouldn't obtain an opportunity you didn't work for. Most of these conservatives enjoy few meaningful privileges themselves and do not work in the corporate sector. Conservatives would be too disgusted to learn about the high salaries 80%'rs are "earning" and complain too much about the lack of output. Corporations do not put up with people who complain about the laziness of others, calling them *toxic*. Instead, they push out *toxic* employees and allow poor performers to underperform continuously. They let some unconnected under-contributors go when the economy weakens, but most just stick around perpetually.

What is merit?

Is the second-generation banker described above, with the proper titles, more than enough years of experience, and the right degree, impressive? With over twenty years of experience and every privilege imaginable in his career, he is still only moderately skilled. Do the quantitative factors prove merit?

What about someone with fewer years of experience but who has exemplified strong judgment, come from nothing, and worked their way up from scratch through sheer skill and effort? If one person started with a silver spoon, has held the proper titles and had the right experiences (given their starting point), but the spoon is now tarnished, is that merit? What if Daddy got them their first job and asked their boss to pump up their resume with consequence-less opportunities where failure could never occur? What if this person doesn't recognize what matters and only receives those opportunities due to Daddy? If hiring these people, how do you know their former title was earned at the other firm and not just gifted to them? I assume the gift in large organizations until I have reason to believe otherwise.

Still on the question of merit, what about a person who started with a plastic spoon made in China but now has a spoon mined from Morenci copper? Copper isn't as lovely as tarnished silver, but at least it's an upgrade from where they started. Do you want the employee who has moved upward or downward from their starting point?

Simply, if President Obama's daughter works as an assistant manager at Chuck E. Cheese's at 40 years old, is that the same as if you or I achieved that title? I would have been thrilled about that role for myself at many points in my life, but it'd be rather unimpressive in Obama's situation.

Does trajectory define merit better than absolute experience?

Merit generally doesn't consider the qualitative factors required to assess trajectory. Therefore, meritocracy (as we typically speak about it) cannot be absolute, or needs to be better defined. (This point focuses on merit in the hiring process. Merit would be known once an employee contributes or fails. Still, we hit the issue of rationalized under-performance for connected employees.)

Conversely, diversity initiatives distort my above point due to their extrapolation of the privilege of the corporate class (i.e., people like my former manager or *Daddy's girl*) onto all white workers. For instance, *white privilege* helps white people hold positions of power and allows poor performers to be hired, keep their jobs, and get promoted. This entirely macro perspective distorts the statistics and completely ignores privilege and nepotism's limited reach only to select candidates. With 330 million people in the U.S., how many hold positions like C-suite, corporate board member, or even VP titles at companies they never started themselves? Relatively few.

Despite being prevalent in large organizations, average white Americans are not meaningfully assisted by nepotism, and privilege is ill-defined by race. Instead, privilege is better defined by a person's starting point (children of a president or life-long banker). Furthermore, the merit of 20%'rs is ignored, and the white privilege point only focuses on select people who happen to be white. It's easy to believe this narrative when 80% of highly-paid workers suck, and most are white. Let's not take the easy path.

Helping these initiatives spread is that many, if not most, corporate employees agree with them. Think about it this way: if you are under-contributing (as an 80%'r), why would you be bothered by non-meritocratic hiring? 80% is a massive proportion of these organizations not working very hard, and these people hold tremendous sway because of the size of the group. Also, suppose you were hired because Daddy called the department head. Why would you be offended if someone was employed for another arbitrary factor like their parent's position, race, or gender? Perhaps espousing these beliefs is a nod to other nepo-babies that you're just like them, born into the right family, and safe from any impact. These white advocates are certainly not giving up their positions to help the disadvantaged. Perhaps diversity initiatives would be unnecessary if organizations solved for nepotism and Pareto's Principle.

All eyes are currently on legacy admissions (i.e., nepotism) at the Ivy League colleges after the Supreme Court struck down race-based admissions as discriminatory. This is where privilege is easily identifiable. A fourth-generation Harvard graduate is very likely to be white because few people of color were admitted 100 years ago. Allowing this preference benefits someone who is merely lucky at the expense of everyone else – whom colleges claim to advocate for (the disadvantaged). Preference provided to legacies allows those students to underperform with fewer opportunities for unconnected

Ch. 15 Nepotism

students. This disproportionately impacts minorities in the macro but absolutely affects all deserving individuals in the micro. Eliminating legacy admissions opens opportunities for all disadvantaged people. But nepotism also exists in the government because it's an easy corruption to cover up in large organizations.

How organizations source candidates:

Senior Management networks → Middle-Manager networks → Individual Contributor networks → The Public.

The further a candidate is from the source (senior management in the above example), the less likely they are to achieve an opportunity. As stated earlier, opportunities for people on the margins only open when elites have exhausted all other options (they've hired all of their friends, or there is more money to be made by expanding opportunities than keeping the wealth to themselves).

Most people believe they are normal, regardless of their situation. The Daddy's girl thinks this is just how people earn their jobs – Daddy calls the boss – and she was not embarrassed to tell me this, probably thinking I was in the same boat (as nepotism is rampant in banking). My former employer sent out a list of prospective borrowers to their employees and asked if anyone knew any relatives of senior management. They demonstrate value to a prospective borrower by hiring that CEO's kid and giving him an inflated salary. They shamelessly explained this plan in the email. This may be a privilege predominantly for those who are white but should not be inferred as a benefit broadly available to white people. The privilege is very narrowly experienced by select people, just like legacy admissions.

When the nepo-babies believe they are normal (and the evidence suggests they are the typical highly paid corporate employee – i.e., normal in the context of large organization leadership), then it is true for them that very few people worked for what they have, their peers are hired into their high-paying corporate job the same way, and there is no such thing as merit. With this perspective, it is easy to understand why corporations sympathize with minorities whom these people believe got a raw deal born into a lack of privilege – which is undeniably true for many minorities. But it extends beyond race or gender. Most Americans are not part of this corporate class; white, black, you name it. As I said, the corporate class is like being royalty, and no, the peasants don't feel better because King Charles shares their skin tone. Only one person can fill a role. Giving it to the undeserving is to take it from everyone who has worked hard.

I had the same privileges (or lack thereof) as my siblings. However, they got stuck in a rut, wishing my parents had done more to help them. They have complained extensively about nepotism and used it as an excuse for not trying harder, progressing, or obtaining what they want. Despite detesting a system that allows others to get more for less, they would rather swap who benefits from such a system than make it more equal – they just wish it worked in their favor. Many more discouraged people join them in waiting for the tides to turn instead of doing what is required.

I have faced many challenges as I learned to navigate the corporate environment. It's not fair that I worked harder than my peers, requiring two associate's degrees, two bachelor's degrees, 15 years of work experience, management experience, and strong performance evaluations everywhere I went just to obtain my first entry-level corporate job, but that's what it

Ch. 15 Nepotism

took. Nepotism is objectively bad for organizations and strong performers, and it is absolutely real, but it is only a hurdle to your career, not a barrier.

My wife had privileges I didn't have that set her up for massive success – her dad finding opportunities in the military, her dad researching the Naval Academy, and her dad helping her with her application. But these things are also available to anyone. Her dad didn't pull strings. He didn't call his buddy, the Senator. And his parents never taught him either. He had to put the time and effort in – he didn't just complain about nepotism or the Senator's son. He had to work for it so his daughter would be better off. Joe Biden had to become VP and later President so his son could prospect bribes from foreign countries.

Someone has to put the time and effort in at some point. The buck stops with you.

Chapter Exercise: Privilege

List the three greatest privileges you received from your family and score how meaningful the privilege is on a scale of 1 to 10 ("10" being Hunter Biden level privilege – i.e., foreign countries that your dad managed affairs for pay you handsomely for consulting on subjects you know little about and/or invest heavily in your firm, the U.S. government allows you to voluntarily resign as a military officer after testing positive for cocaine vs. facing court-martial while your dad is VP, and lastly, using art sales to launder dirty money and/or buy privilege with your dad without the "free press" questioning why a first-time artist can sell paintings to confidential buyers for a half-million dollars only after dad becomes president).

1.   Score: _____

2.   Score: _____

3.   Score: _____

If you scored low on privilege, are you using it as a crutch for your failures? (Y / N)

If you scored high on privilege, are you squandering it? (Y / N)

Chapter 16:

Attribution Bias

An Ivy League business school journal highlighted a not-for-profit credit union as the next big thing in banking. The credit union's flat organizational structure empowered employees closest to the customer (i.e., member) to make decisions by reducing bureaucracy and the all-to-famous line "Let me ask my manager." They trusted their employees and their members and minimized policies and procedures because they hired strong *cultural fits, leaders,* and *entrepreneurs* – no prior experience required. Employees worked in each branch segment so an advisor could help members with cash management one day, a car loan the next, and a mortgage after that. Your advisor was there for you anytime you needed them for whatever you needed them for. They loved their members, and members loved them. They listened to each member's story and made dreams come true. This credit union was nothing like the big banks – a reputation that helped them grow aggressively. Wow. I was inspired to work there.

The reality was that the organization provided no training to employees and threw each one into the weeds on the first day. No mortgage experience? Originate this mortgage! Employees were burdened with unsustainably high levels of work, regularly transferred between departments so that they never gained any expertise in anything, never received any clear guidance, and most employees I met quit within a year. I was by far the longest-term employee in my branch when I left after less than three years with the company. It was reported that mortgage loan demand was so high the IT department was originating loan applications at one point. Why were we so busy?

Per the managers, our members loved us because we were so great. This is literally what one told me once. I asked why are we so great? Because our members loved us! It was very circular and confusing. You can imagine the quality of work expected from an organization whose employees accept such nonsense. But they built an excellent narrative that convinced suckers like me to work there.

One day, a poor couple came in to finalize their car loan. Another "advisor" had pre-approved them, but the borrowers came to me for unknown reasons to complete the loan. The 25-year-old husband and wife couple had over $100,000 in student loans, graduated recently, and still had $10 per hour jobs. The approver was making their dreams come true by approving the loan. Their student loans were on deferment for only another few months, and they qualified for the car loan because the approver excluded that payment. There was no way to afford this loan once the student loan payments kicked in.

Ch. 16 Attribution Bias

Another Member wanted to buy his dream car, a used Land Rover. He made $12 per hour, had a weak credit score, and was lent $40,000 to make his dreams come true.

Another was pre-approved for a 100% cash-out loan against his 16-year-old 1998 Chevy Tahoe. The borrower's credit score was in the mid-500s (very poor, especially for a cash-out deal), and the guy made about $10 per hour. I elevate the situation to my boss. He looks at the details but sees no reason not to fund the loan. I finalized the guy's loan based on his piece of shit truck collateral, the pre-approval, and my manager's guidance.

This borrower never makes a payment before he defaults. The truck didn't run, and he couldn't find a buyer, hence the loan for nearly the entire Blue Book value – what a great idea! He stops by my desk within the first month of the loan and tells me he can't make the first payment. "Come get the truck if you want it" he says. Surprise! Nobody could have foreseen that...

The Land Rover guy didn't make more than a few payments before he defaulted. He blames us for the mistake of giving him an unaffordable loan – and he was absolutely right. He and his banker made material calculation errors when they analyzed the affordability. An organization with any risk management function would have had the sense not to provide this loan (I neither approved nor funded this loan; he needed my help to get out of the situation).

Another member ran a non-profit. He had the bank print off debit cards, and he shipped them to Africa. His "employees" in Africa pulled cash from ATMs. Lots of cash. He comes to me, asks me to print another card, and I tell him the machine is broken. I promptly consulted our compliance department, which shut down his accounts (a surprising action for this organization). Talk about terrorist financing, drug smuggling, or plain old money laundering risk. A year or two earlier, this customer disputed a $12,000 cash withdrawal in Africa, and the bank refunded the money, no questions asked, and continued to print off multiple cards at a time for him. When he complained about the closure, my manager re-opened his account without Compliance's approval.

Another member had millions of dollars deposited in a savings account, earning over 5.00% when accounts only earned 0.05% in 2014. This was 100x the standard return rate.

Were we great just because we were great? Were we great because we had an innovative organizational structure or any other reasons the academic journal promoted? Absolutely not! We didn't help our members. We were a sub-prime lender. We catered to the wealthy for deposits by giving them 100x the regular deposit rate and lent that money out at 7% to subprime borrowers. That was our advantage – doing business no other bank could get away with. I can't explain how the regulators were OK with this. Were they willfully blind?

The middle class got nothing despite credit unions being organized equally for all members' benefit. The middle class has decent credit and income and too modest of savings to individually persuade the organization into a good deal. The middle wants a rate matching their income and credit and won't accept 7% interest on a car loan when they could pay 0-3% elsewhere. Did we approve as many high-quality loans for the core middle class? Not that I saw. I caught flak for trying to approve a $35,000 Jeep Wrangler loan for a couple with 700 credit scores, $80,000 per year income, and minimal other debt. How does that make sense in the context of the $40,000

Land Rover for the guy who made just $25,000 annually and had a score in the 600s? Because we didn't make enough on the middle. If we pay the rich guy 5% on his savings, we cannot lend at 3% to the middle.

This is why the middle class is getting screwed everywhere – neither companies nor politicians make enough off of them. It's why apartments being built are either luxury or "affordable" (i.e., tax-payer subsidized) in most areas.

A bit of real-world experience would have shown the Ivy-League researchers how things actually work. I didn't realize we were a sub-prime lender until after I left – they hired me because I had no perspective and was a total jabroni. They didn't hire employees with experience because those people either would not work there or could not fit into the culture if they learned any bit of risk management at another institution.

Members loved us because we did things other banks wouldn't, like sending numerous debit cards to random people in Africa and letting them take out cash. We ignored money-laundering risk. We gave loans to undeserving or desperate borrowers who couldn't receive a loan from another bank, or worse yet, fraudsters like my 1990s Tahoe borrower. These members immediately told their friends because they found a good deal – a bank that turns a blind eye to risk. The bank grew rapidly. It's easy to grow with no standards. If your goals involve sleeping with many partners, how easily could you inflate those figures if you dropped all standards and concepts of risk? If you want to make a lot of money tomorrow, ignore all the risks of a life of crime and advertise your services for drug dealing, smuggling, hit jobs, prostitution, etc. But it's easy to imagine the repercussions of a life of crime, even though the concept is the same – excessive risk is their competitive advantage.

The leadership team who implemented this culture was removed one day without notice, less than two years after that business journal study. The culture was verifiably unsustainable. To this day, the journal does not appear to have studied management's failure. Hmmm… But it's not just businesses that are misleading.

American media stories about Venezuela's "socialist success" started appearing in the early to mid-2010s. These media lacked perspective, attributed the success to the socialist economy, and failed to dig into why this country was becoming prosperous – it's oil-rich, benefiting from high oil prices. When oil prices crashed in 2015, the country couldn't sustain itself, and its people have faced devastation – lacking food, medical supplies, prescription drugs, and pretty much everything else. The people are trying desperately to flee in any way they can. This short-lived "success" proved nothing favorable about socialism. Socialism wasn't why it worked – temporarily high oil revenues supported their system. But that was a fantastic narrative to sell the American Left. Venezuela's success also lasted less than a few years. No surprises there.

Remember my story about taking excessive risk in the 2000s or Jay Gajavelli's empire? How long did "success" last for those participants? Just a few years. False narratives are unsustainable. (Beware: Governments can support false narratives for much longer due to the essentially unlimited resources. However, Venezuela shows that even governments are vulnerable to sudden changes in the environment.)

Years ago, a friend of mine was in a similar stage of reskilling and entering a new career. Every time I saw him, he had just received another raise. He started at $30K per year, but within a few months, it was $45K, then $60K, then $80K, then $100K+. He bragged about how much his company loved him, and they'll do anything to keep him. I started feeling bad about myself because my salary hadn't improved much. "How's he so much better than me?" runs through my head. Then his girlfriend starts doing the same thing. OK, now I'm calling BS. Not because she didn't deserve it, but c'mon... About three years into his role, he tells me he's switching careers because his job requires a lot of math, and it's too much effort to learn.

It hits me. No one knows how much I make until I tell them (I'm a slow learner, and scheming is not in my blood). We can have an idea of people's earnings by what they buy – their house, neighborhood, cars, toys, vacations, etc. But no one actually knows until you tell them. And you often add 20%. You can also pull various levers to increase your spending power: credit cards, loans, working overtime for a period, leaving regular employment with solid benefits to "consult" on your own, and decreasing your tax withholdings – this last one is pervasive and very dangerous. I came across many prospective borrowers looking for a loan to pay their income taxes because they temporarily reduced their withholdings to increase their cash flow. This could turn into a destructive debt cycle because if you can't afford to pay your taxes today, what will change that allows you to pay them later, plus the new loan?

People could also be trust-fund babies. You just do not know, and their success may be a façade. Think of it this way: would you rather tell people you live on Mommy and Daddy's dime or that you run a successful business that nobody can disprove? It's funny how much leisure time all these young entrepreneurs have while established business owners work more than full-time until their 60s or 70s.

A friend of a friend runs an e-commerce company that is apparently quite successful. He lived the high life near the best beaches for a bit, resided in a $1.5 million condo when I met him, hired several of his friends to work for him temporarily, and had money to spend all the time. He was successful by any economic measure. I talk to him about his business – what drives growth and users? Facebook ads. That's it. He attributes his entire success to Facebook Ads. Is this guy incredibly knowledgeable about advertising, marketing, or sales? Did he have extensive experience doing this for another employer and learn best practices? Nope. He says he just figured it out on the job. Are Facebook ads really that effective? I cannot find any data to support his claim. I have banked hundreds of successful companies, none of which attribute their success to Facebook ads or advertising in general.

I check out his website. To be blunt, it looks like a scam, and to this day, I have no idea if it is legit. A video ad includes a charismatic guy telling the viewer to click the link and subscribe to your no-obligation trial over and over again, hardly mentioning what you're subscribing to. It's also geared toward the elderly, which is another red flag.

All of his friends are enamored by his success and kiss his ass. They are inspired to start their own companies and follow his lead – just buy some Facebook ads. Oh, and Tai Lopez's social media training and a few lottery tickets while they're at it.

One day, he discloses that his dad is the Chief Financial Officer at a bank. Things start making more sense.

Ch. 16 Attribution Bias

What is the most likely scenario: (a) This 29-year-old college drop-out is a business wizard who cracked the code, which, believe it or not, is to just buy Facebook Ads, (b) It's the scam it appears to be, or (c) He's a trust-fund baby living off of Daddy's money?

I very much doubt (a) is the reason. Even if the company is legit, how do we know the secret to his success isn't just that Daddy pumps unlimited resources into his advertising, and the actual return on investment (ROI) is dog-shit? Market anything enough, and it will sell, but ROI is a constraint for most companies. I just don't know. Am I jealous? Absolutely, but I still won't start a company thinking I can replicate it, and neither should you when you come across a similar situation. This guy won the lottery, no matter what the actual cause of success is.

The ability to replicate the success you admire is essential. You cannot replicate winning the lottery. You can only buy a ticket and play the extremely low probabilities. That is not how successful businesses are built. If you start a company thinking Facebook Ads are a panacea, you will be out of business unless Daddy buys the ads for you. You just can't replicate the success in these scenarios through anything other than massive funding or pure chance. And the chance is abysmal.

Likewise, does learning to play guitar really well increase your chances of becoming a famous musician? Yes. It increases your chances from 0% to 0.000002%. Good luck! Is that meaningful enough to put your energy toward that goal? Are you thinking, "But I'm special!"? Chances are you're probably not special. I am not special either – it's OK.

If you love music, do not stop because I tell you you're not special! Do it because you want to do it. If you become successful, great! Not everything we do needs to make money. My monetary and time investment in remodeling my home is not resulting in value appreciation. The market is softening, and my house has lost significant value despite more and more upgrades. It doesn't make financial sense, but I do it because I like it, I get better with each project, and the home becomes more comfortable. Do your thing because you enjoy it! You'll be much happier in the long run.

I want to stop here and clarify the use of statistics. It is a common misconception that if 1 in 10 people develop something, let's say, becoming a rich and famous musician, that a person then has a 10% chance of becoming a rich and famous musician. This is absolutely incorrect on the individual level. You may have a 0% chance or a 100% chance, which depends entirely on you as an individual. The only thing the statistic suggests is that if you pick 10 people at random out of a population, one might become famous, or extrapolate the information to 10% of the population might become famous. If you feel extra optimistic, you may say there are 10 opportunities to become famous for every 100 people. And that may even be an overly generous assumption given the connected/nepotistic nature of this and many other industries. The statistics have no bearing on you, the individual.

A more practical way of thinking about this may be to consider Boxing Champion Mike Tyson. If Mike Tyson picks a fight with a random, similarly sized male on the street, are his chances 50/50 he wins/loses? No. It is roughly 100% certain that he wins because he is a boss who has worked extremely hard to become as good as he is.

So, when I say your chances go from 0% to 0.000002% to become a famous musician, I broadly speak to all readers

Ch. 16 Attribution Bias

because I do not know each person's situation and assume that my audience represents a roughly random sample and the selection is also random. Although, I choose to reiterate here: your chances of becoming a rock star are still abysmal unless your Daddy is Paul McCartney or Rick Ruben. And if either of them is Daddy, your chances are closer to 100%, just like if you were Mike Tyson in a street fight. Even Rob Schneider's daughter has made a career in show business.

So, let's take the highly generous interpretation of the statistic and assume there are a few open positions for celebrities; you better get in line behind Rob Schneider, Paul McCartney, Rick Ruben, Mike Tyson, Connor McGregor, Will Ferrel, Bruce Willis, Will Smith, and on and on as they promote their relatives and friends first. If there's any leftover room, you just roll the dice and wait with the other ten million dreamers without connections. Not to say it can't happen; it's just not going to. Best of luck.

For all I know, the e-commerce website is legit, and the success is due to hard work and knowledge the owner is unwilling to share. His friends are still listening to his story and trying to replicate his business with the information he communicates. But, it's impossible to replicate without understanding the actual cause, which is the practical application of understanding attribution. If you do not understand the source of the success, you cannot replicate it.

The same low probability and lack of replicability apply to winner-take-all industries like music, producing, filmmaking, acting, influencing, and many more, where equally talented individuals compete for a single top spot (or minimal numbers of top positions). And even if a person is skilled enough to beat Mike Tyson in a fight, it says nothing about the ability to achieve the same level of fame and fortune.

You can't replicate the kid who became a millionaire by opening Lego boxes on YouTube – many have tried to copy it, but he won the lottery. Further, you have no idea what YouTube's algorithm is. For all you know, that kid is the nephew of a programmer who put in the code to promote this kid's videos.

Think that's outrageous? See the HBO documentary *McMillions* about how executives got the right McDonald's Monopoly pieces to their friends and families to win the million-dollar prize year after year. Did you have a 1 in 600,000,000 chance of winning the million dollars, as advertised? No, you had a 0% chance. Not because 0.0000002% is so low, but because their organization was corrupt. Think of all the nepotism and corruption in the world. Do you think people who can make or break millionaires aren't using it to their advantage when there is little-to-no oversight? Executives hand out the winning Monopoly pieces to family. Banking leaders hand out six- figure salaries to their friend's kids. Still, all social media companies, coders, and developers have stronger ethics despite much more money at stake?

How did the FBI find the fraud with McDonald's Monopoly? Statistics, as the investigators determined the (im)probability that multiple winners could be connected to the company.

*Technically, McDonald's executives did not run the scheme. They outsourced handling of the pieces to a firm called Simon Marketing. Still, when the stakes are high, and oversight is nil, corruption is certain.

Ch. 16 Attribution Bias

Chapter Exercise: Attribution

Given your inside knowledge of your employer, why is your organization successful?

___

Employer's stated cause of success:

___

Does your reason align with their stated reasons? (Y / N)

Chapter 17:

Join the Military

You may be wondering why I am writing a chapter about joining the military in a book marketed towards veterans. Just trust me. Turn around and march right back into the recruiter or your commanding officer's office and beg for them to take you back. You'll thank me later.

Most people look back at their military years fondly on the experiences, the purpose, and the friendships they developed. If not you, someone in your family has probably served in the military.

My wife and nearly her entire immediate family have served: Grandpa, Dad, brother, sister, and herself. Both of my grandpas served, an uncle, an aunt, and myself. None of these people regret their service. In fact, my grandpa grew up so poor he wanted anything to escape. He enlisted in the Army at 14; they discovered his age and kicked him out. At 18, he re-enlisted and served in Japan after World War II, helping to

Ch. 17 Join The Military

rebuild the country. He was a hard son-of-a-bitch that took no shit from anybody and had a massive problem with authority. This is probably why he didn't stay in longer than one enlistment.

I never connected better with him than after I enlisted. He didn't regret his time and looked back fondly in his later years. Once I enlisted, he started telling stories about serving in Japan and sending love letters to my grandma while away, things I never heard previously. I don't believe he saw much action in the theater, but as a Private, he had to physically threaten a First Sergeant to be repaid on a loan he made, acting unofficially as a pay-day lender to other enlisted. Perhaps banking is in my blood...

I find it bizarre there are entire families in America who have been here for generations and have never served. No grandparents, no uncles, no parents, no children, nothing. WWI, WWII, Korea, Vietnam, Desert Storm, Iraqi Freedom – these families missed them all. Many are well-to-do families. Perhaps it's time to break the mold if it has been a few generations.

I don't have regrets in my life, but leaving the Air Force is about the closest thing to a regret I feel. I do very well now, much better than I would be doing if I stayed in, but it was a long road. I don't think I've yet broken even, and the impact I've made in the private sector is much less significant.

I'm trying to provide a framework for life here, but that's what the military does. The military trains you and provides job requirements, study materials, standards and policies to understand, performance evaluation metrics, and promotion requirements. When I left the military, I didn't know what mattered and had no framework for how the private sector worked. My parent's advice was to go to college and work hard, but that wasn't the answer, or at least not the entire answer. A college education is only the tip of the iceberg; there's so much more to get right. Or, perhaps more importantly, not to get wrong. Because of this, I struggled in my personal life and career and would have been better off learning a trade than going to college for a nonsense art degree. Also, instead of continuing to serve, what did I do? Nothing meaningful in a macro sense except learning the lessons that allowed me to write this book. I hope this has an impact, but it's very uncertain at this time (and improbable).

This is not to say the military doesn't have its challenges – members risk their lives every day. I worked in Public Affairs and never deployed overseas. I didn't do more, which I now wish I did. My wife deployed as a line officer and served in war. Despite having a very tough role as a "Nuke," she loved it. She never knew anything different as she went to the academy directly out of high school at 17. She is now becoming well aware of the unrewarding private sector. Many veterans don't like the rules, regulations, and hierarchy of the military. However, they do train you, something most employers won't do (and what my hipster brother has been waiting for his entire life in the private sector). They also tell you everything you must do to do well, earn a promotion, and build a successful career. Job security is the highest of any industry. Pay is good, too. My salary was only $25,000 per year before I left active duty (they now pay much more), but I got free housing, a food allowance, and no-cost healthcare. Total compensation was over $50,000 per year, there were zero job requirements before joining, and they trained me. It took me six years after separating to earn the equivalent in the private sector, and I had to work two jobs to get it, not to mention the heartache as I struggled to make it on my own.

Ch. 17 Join The Military

I was enlisted. My wife was an officer. She (and her siblings) went to the U.S. Naval Academy – the best Engineering college in the world. Her sister received a Bachelor of Science in English. That's an unheard-of degree – English degrees are usually Bachelor of Arts. I've slandered arts degrees enough – I won't go there again – but the critical difference between an Arts and Science degree is the math intensity. Math is the difference between low and high pay in any sector. The Naval Academy requires extensive math, no matter the degree. That's substantial.

My wife obtained a free, world-class education and a high-paying job after graduating. Starting salaries for Officers are currently over $40,000 plus housing ($15,000 to $30,000 depending on location) plus food ($2,000-$3,000) plus world-class benefits ($10,000 - $20,000, including tuition reimbursement, healthcare, VA loans, GI Bill). This puts total cash compensation between $55,000 to $75,000 and total compensation at $65,000 to $95,000 in your first year! In addition, you may be eligible for a bonus depending on your career field, and your earnings are tax-free if overseas (add ~30% to your pay – i.e., *gross-up*). You also receive regular raises with time in service and making rank. There are almost no private sector jobs with that level of pay and as much certainty of progression.

Military service is not just about the quantifiable benefits; you gain perspective. If you hate America or feel like America hates you, you've been left behind, or whatever, then you should join (assuming you are American. Ignore this advice if you're not...). Humble yourself and understand the military will treat you like an equal – an equal piece of dirt – but equal. Marines say, "Only one color matters to the Marines: Green." No woke corporation can provide as much equity, and the

Ch. 17 Join The Military

Marines are far more racially diverse. Experience what centuries of sustained tradition and culture can offer you if you're willing to learn and care for something beyond yourself. The military is a direct path out of the lower socio- economic classes, and that path is never blocked by the boss' nephew or an organization that secretly wants you to fail. The military wants you to succeed and provides every resource available; you just need to put in the work.

You also get a sense of purpose. Purpose matters. I earlier discussed my lack of caring about school and the easy classes I took – I never felt that way in the Air Force. I studied the Air Force Standard, my job, and took my role very seriously. I begged my leaders to send me to SERE training (I never got to go). I was stationed at Davis-Monthan Air Force Base in Tucson, Arizona, with the 355th Fighter Wing, home to the 12th Air Force / Air Forces Southern Command. They managed South American Operations. We also had Customs and Border Protection (CBP) on base. My manager, Sergeant Lohr, set up a flight to the border with CBP due to my interest. He was a good manager. The Air Force still uses my photographs for recruiting more than a decade later, and the HH-60 Helicopter Wikipedia page had used one of my photos for years. Few achieve that kind of lasting impact in the private sector, myself included.

I was also paid to assist in the production of various films on base, including *Transformers II: Revenge of the Fallen*, starring Shia Labeouf, Meghan Fox, and John Turturro. I shared a taxi from the production site with John Turturro and had a pleasant exchange with him – he's an incredibly down- to-earth guy. I also met Olivia Wilde, Bryan Cranston, and other stars on different projects.

Ch. 17 Join The Military

I never cared much about the wars in Afghanistan and Iraq. Is terrorism a threat that needs to be neutralized? Yes. But I joined because the military is an essential function, regardless of whatever war is taking place. The 12th Air Force served a critical role in managing South American operations: drug smuggling, human trafficking, development, and area relations. Working for the wing Public Affairs unit on base, the 12th Air Force asked me to go on a three-month deployment with the commanding General. He was planning a diplomatic tour in the Caribbean and Latin America, meeting with their political leaders and top military brass. New managers took over my office by this time and were very unsupportive. They worked to promote their own careers, and doing favors for their staff wasn't something they considered – they wouldn't let me go, despite the personal request from a higher command.

Later, I applied for a special duty assignment near the end of my active-duty enlistment. It was with the POW/MIA Accountability Task Force. This group seeks out Prisoners of War and those Missing in Action from old wars who were never found. They send scouts to former war zones to find wreckage sites and camps to bring the service members home. This unit has an amazing mission, and I hoped to support them as best I could. Unfortunately, I wasn't selected for this either.

The Air Force afforded me many incredible opportunities despite not obliging to every opportunity presented. Not being selected was discouraging at the moment and weighed on my decision to leave, but I only missed out because there are abundant unique opportunities in the military – experiences you will never obtain in the private sector. Will you ever stare down an Iranian dinghy in the Strait of Hormuz? Will your private sector employer send you to Syracuse University to earn a degree while paying you a salary with living expenses? Are blockbuster films produced at your office? Probably not. Sure, I had some bad managers, but bad managers exist everywhere. My worst managers have been in the private sector. I should have had a better perspective about what awaited me outside the military. I was wrong about the private sector being better in any way except general safety.

My brother-in-law is an F-18 fighter pilot, has been to war, and has lost friends in service. That is not the same service I experienced, so it is easier for me to talk about staying in. In November 2019, he considered leaving the military to work for the airlines. Despite the hardening experience, he and his friends were considering leaving primarily for the financial benefits of the private sector. Mind you, these are O-4s with 10+ years of experience in the military wanting to leave the military for private-sector salaries. Their base pay was over $90,000 per year plus housing, food, flight pay, and bonus – they were earning more than $150,000 per year as 33-year-olds in the military! They had done some homework and knew the union airline pilot job starting pay was significantly less, but they thought they'd be millionaires in no time.

Apparently, there is a massive campaign to make our servicemembers believe all civilians are wealthy and service members are being financially screwed. I thought this when I left nearly 15 years ago, and most of my peers had expressed the same. Private sector success is often a myth, and as you're probably aware (unless you're in currently), becoming and maintaining millionaire status is very rare. Hell, it's hard just to hit the six figures consistently. Most separating members tell a

Ch. 17 Join The Military 215

story of a friend-of-a-friend who makes $150,000 per year after separating but only made $30,000 base pay while in. As stated previously, this person either won the lottery of jobs, is just a made-up tale, or has extensive connections to the company offering such a salary. That achievement is not replicable (there are too few high-paying positions relative to those separating). If you have limited connections, you are more likely to experience something like I did, where you financially struggle without direction – which is why I wrote this book.

My officer wife was adamant that she could have easily made six figures after separating instead of going to medical school, and she had many examples of others who had done the same. Or, so she thought. One friend was an unemployed teacher moving from one temporary position to the next; another worked in sales and told her he earned $80,000 per year (deduct 20% for exaggeration/ego, and he was probably making $65K). $65K or $80K per year are respectable incomes, but they're significantly less than military officer pay and even worse when the cash value of military benefits are considered (which are always meaningfully better than private sector benefits).

I would have encouraged her to stay in if I had known her at the time. Fortunately, I was able to convince her brother to stay in. He receives his flight pay, a $35,000 per year bonus, and is earning nearly $200K when total cash compensation is considered. That pay is essentially guaranteed for any fighter pilot with the same years of experience.

Comradery, security, skills, connections, purpose, and pay are all provided. You need to take the first step, and four years is a short time to give it a try. Ignore the success narratives

Ch. 17 Join The Military

of the private sector, and you will likely enjoy yourself.

Pro-Tip: You must disregard the power-belly chapter if you choose to join. The military tends to look down on large bellies unless you're a Senior NCO in the Air Force…

Ch. 17 Join The Military

Chapter Exercise: Military

Note the veterans in your family. If able, talk to them about their experience.

1.

2.

3.

4.

5.

Chapter 18:

Leadership

We know Leadership is more than being charismatic or a con artist who can convince others to do their bidding. We know organizations misuse the word and use it in place of *follower* or *connected* (due to the all-too-often selection of "leaders" based on nepotism). Let's move past how others use the term and drill down to the essence of what it is and/or what it should be.

Does a leader sell out their people? No. A leader must be trusted by their staff. A leader is a representative of their group to upper management and a representative of upper management to their group. They must balance the organization's goals with their employees' goals and capabilities. This does not occur in many organizations.

For example, you're a middle manager. Your staff has been working overtime and complaining about conditions and work-life balance, but upper management won't give you

Ch. 18 Leadership

additional resources to relieve the burden. Attrition may also be horrendous. What do you do? Most (bad) managers will force those conditions on their employees and say they can do nothing – deal with it perpetually.

That is not good enough.

My wife's residency program had this problem. The program's 21 residents were gas-lit, broken, and beaten. Her class started residency in 2020 just as COVID broke out, working the first year as general hospitalists during the peak (think ICU, inpatient care, etc.) – just imagine the anxiety of newly minted physicians starting to practice during this time. This was also the same period when the Phoenix metropolitan area was growing by hundreds of thousands of new residents, certainly increasing patient flows in the heart of the city where they practiced. Another program in the area grew its staff by nearly 70% to handle the burden. Her program maintained the same level of staffing. Her class tried talking to management multiple times to address their fatigue. Many of them had often considered quitting. Leadership told them, "We hear you, and we're working on it." Months passed, then a year, and leadership never instituted meaningful changes. The residents raised concerns, and management squashed them repeatedly.

One day, a resident stops showing up. Nobody knows what happened except that leadership rescheduled her most challenging shifts on the remaining group. The residents had been telling leadership how little capacity they had for over a year, but no action was taken to mitigate the burden, and leadership even continued to pile on more. A group of residents and their husbands meet up, and the residents talk about quitting, but they refuse to take a stand for fear of conflict.

They're so beaten and hopeless that they have no fight left.

The following week, we come together, and conversations start up again. One resident tells everyone leadership will "fire us if we raise concerns; they've done it before." Another resident confirms her remarks.

I'm pissed. I never underestimate a lousy manager, but if you're so concerned about retaliation, then why are you complaining? To rile everyone up and then tell them there's nothing they can do is horse shit. My fears for their mental health deepen.

I sit on this conversation for a day before it eats at me and escalate my concerns to the national residency governing body. I explain the fear of retaliation, the missing resident, the recently deteriorated morale, and my fear that the discouraged group is at risk due to their hopelessness and noted increased risk-taking.

The national residency governing body contacts the organization immediately, and management (not program leadership) starts digging into concerns. My wife contacts the absent resident to inform her I'm elevating the situation and that she may be contacted about the issues.

That resident informs us she attempted suicide after growing hopeless with the program, which is why she was absent.

This was my greatest fear.

Did leadership ever contact the remaining residents to see how they're doing? No. Did leadership schedule a stand-down, where the team takes a day or so to recharge? Nope. After she attempted suicide, all leadership did was take her most brutal

Ch. 18 Leadership

shifts and reschedule them on the remaining residents.

Someone tried killing themselves after trying to work with this leadership team and growing hopeless, and the only action managers took was to reschedule her shifts on the remaining group.

This really eats at me over time because, in the same month that resident attempted suicide, another resident under this leadership team died after getting lost on a hike. Mind you, this is not a large team under this management – 21 residents, that's all.

This death/near-death rate is almost impossible through random chance.

If not likely through random chance, then we look for a common factor – the residency program.

I've never seen anything like this in over 20 years working in large organizations. I doubt you have, either.

10% faced death in the same month. What are the chances of two out of 21 otherwise healthy 30-year-olds dying in the same month through behavior-driven activities (neither fell ill)?

You may think I am ridiculous for connecting a hiking death in Arizona to this program – bear with me a moment. It is actually incredibly rare for hikers to die. Especially hikers in their early 30s. 4.5 million people live in Maricopa County (where the hiker lived and died), and we get 16 million visitors yearly – many of them hikers. 378 people died in 2021 (most recent data available at the time of this writing, and most of them are over age 50). It's hard to be precise, but the probability is less than a millionth of a percent that one of the hikers is part of this group. He was only 31.

Alone, the hiking death is tragic but does not appear connected to the program. I never thought anything of the connection until well after I heard the other resident attempted suicide in the same month. This was also in the same month, mind you, that I became so worried that I elevated concern about the group's mental health due to hopelessness and observable increased risk-taking. Isn't it conceivable that the first resident died on the hike due to a lack of preparedness, given his mental state after working at this organization that overworks, neglects, and gas-lights its employees? There certainly are connecting factors.

Did the program stand down when this resident died? No. Did they reach out to the team individually to check in? No. After months of complaints from residents and a peer dying, leadership just took his hardest shifts and put them on the remaining residents. That other resident attempted suicide three weeks later.

Roughly 1 in 300 people attempt suicide. That's far too common, and I hope everyone is strong enough to request help when needed. However, a group of 21 residents suggests this should occur about once every 15 years. The hiking- related death should only happen once every several hundred years with a group of this size. These events occurred in the same month with a group of 21 otherwise healthy young people and should essentially never happen together by random chance.

I hope you see the connection now.

(A more accurate analysis may be to generalize the death rate for the age group from behavior-driven events. It is not included here for simplicity, as complicating the calculation does not materially change the improbability.)

Ch. 18 Leadership

But residency is supposed to be tough, right?

Fuck off. OK. I've been spouting hard work this entire book. My Naval Nuclear Engineer turned Medical Doctor wife understands hard work. There's a difference here.

In the 2022 Netflix film Pale Blue Eye, Christian Bale's character investigates a suicide at the West Point military academy. The Commanders are notably concerned and acknowledge they're supposed to push the students to their limits – this is how they develop the best officers – but they need to know when to stop. This is just a movie, but the sentiment is confirmed by the military officers in my own family. Even one person dying is a big flippin' deal. Two (outside of war), and leaders are losing their jobs. You cannot just push and push and push, and when people break, you just continue to push. That makes you a sadist. Or, in our case, apparently just a residency program director at Barrow Neurological Institute. Awful.

I tell you this story because this is not leadership. Pushing people after their breaking point makes you a bad person. Is the organization to blame? Upper management was never aware of the problem. Program Leadership apparently never informed upper management about a crisis brewing (probably why they were never allocated additional staff). Upper management acted as soon as they found out, and things got better for the group as they instituted meaningful changes. I wouldn't hold my breath expecting improvements to persist. Companies that run this way (neglect employees) always screw people over – it's their competitive advantage.

This is an example of leadership as a management function, but leadership extends beyond management. Leadership is also about vision. Is vision always world-changing? No, you don't have to be Elon Musk to be a visionary. Vision could be as simple as conceptually understanding your job or function well enough to take the reins when all goes to hell.

According to my F-18 pilot brother-in-law, the Boeing airplane crashes of recent years were caused by a software glitch. We all heard this. We also heard these crashes occurred in 3rd world countries – it wasn't American pilots. Why didn't American flights crash if we were using the same software?

What we didn't hear is that pilots from foreign countries are not like American commercial pilots. They have limited experience, and their pilot training is far less rigorous. When everything goes well and works as planned, they know how to fly because they rely on the software to fly the plane. When things do not go well, they crash, and everyone on board dies. Automation is required to work well for them to fly safely. American flights rely on software, too, but the pilots know how the plane operates without automation and have flown many missions manually – most pilots come from the military. This is why we hear about American pilots landing a plane after catastrophic engine failure, as is the case of Navy veteran fighter pilot Tammie Jo Shults on Southwest Flight 1380. We also have two of these guys (or gals) on each flight, something they may not have overseas. This is also why we should be cautious about automation – we need professionals – but that's another topic.

The conceptual understanding of your specialty is leadership. This is why our pilots are the best, and when things go awry, they can still land a plane. The event that the software malfunctions and the plane crashes doesn't happen on commercial flights in America. The U.S. has not had a fatal commercial plane crash in nearly 15 years, despite the 737 Max flying extensively in the U.S. with faulty software.

Related to the odds of two medical residents facing death in the same month (of 21 total residents total), two 737 Max crashes globally resulted in the grounding of all flights with that plane model, despite the probability of a single casualty being so much lower with millions of flight hours logged. Yet a 10% near-death rate wasn't significant enough for Barrow Neurological Institute's managers to take any action.

On a less sophisticated but equally valid level, a professional photographer who uses a high-tech DSLR camera can be a leader. The camera may not produce as high- quality images as your auto-adjusted phone or Instagram filter, but the photographer knows perspective, lighting, color, framing, depth, and other vital concepts. They know how to program their camera and have the full scope of the job, i.e., perspective or conceptual understanding of everything, not just factors that make themselves look best in a selfie. If Instagram filters go offline, the influencer cannot influence. If your iPhone battery dies or auto-functions break, your pictures are likely crap. A real photographer knows how to adjust, fix the settings, and take an outstanding photo in nearly any circumstance – not only under perfect conditions.

In the world of finance, many bankers have never experienced an economic downturn. When bankers are confronted by the demands for loan portfolio growth vs. the riskiness of a prospective borrower, many vastly underestimate the risk when a company has performed well during the peak economy. Bankers will assume the growth trajectory during the boom will last indefinitely into the future. In reality, *normalization* tends to occur, a more modest growth or mid-cycle performance (in neither boom nor bust conditions) – which bankers and the companies themselves fail to foresee, and why most mergers and acquisitions destroy company value.

Over the past several years, companies leveraged up on peak economy cash flows that were unsustainable. Regulators are now anticipating many of these deals to sour and result in more significant losses than originally anticipated. Commercial bankers who can only handle the peak economy will fade away just like the mortgage bankers of yesteryear. The ones who can handle fledgling and enduring companies are best equipped for long-term success.

A life-long career, or one at the whim of the cycles?

When we say we need more leaders, this is what we should mean. Leadership is not unquestioning optimism, nor is it performing tasks someone else has developed into a system. You must be able to recognize failures and take control when systems fail, and they all fail eventually.

Vision also entails having obtained enough perspective to know what matters (i.e., sufficient experience and education to develop the necessary values). The primary business functions are an excellent example of competing interests (i.e., values) – Marketing/Sales, Finance/Accounting, Supply Chain/Operations, and Technology. A leader's responsibility is to balance those interests. Most people specialize in one area and work in that specialty their entire life. Some work their way laterally to gain a broader perspective. The top-level leaders, the C-Suite, include the Chief Financial Officer (CFO), Chief Operating Officer (COO), Chief Marketing Officer (CMO), Chief Technology Officer (CTO), and in banks the Chief Risk Officer (CRO), Chief Credit Officer (CCO), or Chief Investment Officer (CIO). There are also a few newer titles like Chief Diversity Officer, Chief Accounting Officer, and Chief Administrative Officer. Bankrupt companies often have a Chief Restructuring Officer responsible for finding ways to improve cash flow, cut unnecessary costs, and increase overall value to creditors (although rare, this position will become more prominent in the near future, which is why I include it).

Responsibilities and perspectives vary depending on the C-Suite specialization; each is the respective expert and leader of their function. The CFO ensures accurate reporting and that the business has the funds to operate and grow. The COO ensures manning, planning, procurement, product development, and general operating capacity are well utilized and capable of meeting production goals. The CMO ensures appropriate brand messaging, sales, and product placement. The CTO ensures the management information systems are sufficient, maintained, and upgraded when needed. This is obviously not all-inclusive and very generalized, but you get a sense of the responsibilities.

These executives report to the CEO. The CEO started in a particular specialty and worked her way up. The resilience required to earn the CEO title may be why many have served in a sales function earlier in their careers. Sophisticated sales roles require that you work with different internal departments to better understand your product to meet customer demands, along with handling competing interests (making the sale vs. achieving sufficient margin), thus broadening their perspective. The CEO takes the facts and perspectives provided by the above specialties and combines them with her values and the organization's goals to create a roadmap. She needs to be aware of the capabilities and constraints of the organization. Perhaps the CFO has advised that the company cannot obtain the funding required for 200% expansion, so growth must be reduced to only 20%. The CEO needs to balance goals and reality and perhaps shift resources by prioritizing initiatives. This comes by knowing what is of relative value and acknowledging not everything matters equally.

In commercial banking, sales and risk work as a team. These are called Relationship Managers and Portfolio Managers/Underwriters. These are your CEO/CFO equivalents. The Relationship Managers (i.e., Sales)develop a marketing plan and a strategy. They work with Portfolio Managers (i.e., Risk) to understand the constraints of their strategy. For example, the bank cannot lend to hedge funds, start-ups, drug cartels, or even as simply as the borrower must meet specific metrics. The bank's policies and guidance define lending criteria, considering the local environment. The board of directors – i.e., the investors and owners of the bank - set the risk appetite. The bank cannot lend infinitely. The bank has capital constraints based on regulatory requirements and funds on hand. They need to use discretion to whom they lend, not only because of risk but because of efficient allocation. If you lend all your capital to low-risk, low-reward customers, what will you do when an acceptably higher-risk, higher-reward borrower shows up? Not lend and receive low returns perpetually? Perhaps, if that is the strategy decided upon.

Alternatively, in the case of my credit union paying 5% to some wealthy depositors, can they afford to lend at less than 5%? No, they cannot.[1] This involves structuring a portfolio with a mix of different borrowers and capital sources – something the Sales team cannot perform independently.

If the environment involves increased risk-taking, the Sales function will override Risk. This was seen in recent years as

---

[1] (They would use a weighted average cost to determine their minimum lending rate, but this is simplified to illustrate the point more clearly.)

funding was ample and banks eased requirements to compete effectively. Should they keep capital idle when risks increase? There is an opportunity cost for lack of action and investors will pull their funds. A leader must weigh the strategy's costs/benefits or risks/rewards. Perhaps risks are past a point of no return, and the company is screwed in any scenario, so the only option is to keep taking on more and more risk (and keep those bonuses large) until the bubble pops. Or, the government just printed $9 trillion, so tell your friends to come on down to Noah's Lending Emporium Extravaganza!

A key lesson on balance is learned from the COVID-19 pandemic. The U.S. followed Dr. Anthony Fauci's lead on the pandemic. He knew the most and was the authoritative expert on viruses and public health – this is a fact. He followed the facts and *the science*. When the science told him masks were ineffective, he followed *the science*. When the science told him masks were effective, he followed *the science*. When the science suggested perhaps three masks were necessary, he followed *the science* no matter how ridiculous this was. He paid attention to the facts and recommended (pressed the government to enforce) mandates on the public due to concerns driven by *the science*. Common sense, individual liberties, and traditional American values were disbanded due to the unprecedented events requiring us to follow *the science*, despite *the science* and our understanding of the situation changing rapidly.

Much of the early COVID "disinformation" has been found to be true, but we limited speech in the name of fighting the virus. Fauci's narratives fell apart within a few years – just like our fragile investor narratives. COVID vaccine mandates occurred on healthy adults, despite limited research and lack of FDA approval at the time. I am not an anti-vax'r. I'm pro- science. I want my vaccine studied before the government requires vaccination. Initial reports of the dangers of the vaccine were banned on social media due to "disinformation" with the help of government agencies flagging undesirable posts. We now know the vaccines do increase the risk of myocarditis in young men. Young men are not at meaningful risk of death from COVID unless they have a co-morbidity, and the real science showed this early on with deaths concentrated with those over age 65.[8]

Newer studies show that acquired immunity is at least as effective as the vaccine, but it was also known by using common sense. The vaccines have hardly been shown to reduce transmission given the extensive cases of vaccinated individuals acquiring COVID, but the government tells healthy young people they just need more shots and it'll work next time, and on and on. Some countries have halted COVID vaccination of young children due to the risks outweighing the benefits to an individual, but the U.S. hasn't because mandates here have focused more on the benefits to the greater good over the detriment to any individual receiving the vaccine. By this writing, the pandemic is over, and nobody seriously considers more shots any longer because... *the science.*

---

[8] (2020, October 23). Race, Ethnicity, and Age Trends in Persons Who Died from COVID-19 — United States, May–August 2020. Centers for Disease Control and Prevention. Retrieved July 26, 2023, from
https://www.cdc.gov/mmwr/volumes/69/wr/mm6942e1.htm.

Ch. 18 Leadership

Dr. Fauci also worked to shut down talk of "conspiracies" about the pandemic originating from a lab leak in China. The FBI and other intelligence agencies have now confirmed this is the most likely story of the virus' origination. We will never know with 100% certainty, but even Jon Stewart had some common sense when he stated in 2021 that the virus came from a town with a lab with the same name as the freaking virus! Of course, it did! I don't need a report from the FBI to prove this. I hope you didn't either, but many people did and still don't believe it. This is the problem with educated people – they're too smart for their own good. You follow *the science*, great! Do you also have common sense? No. *The science* hasn't proven you are intelligent, so you must wait for the experts to tell you what to think.

Why did Fauci not want to talk about the virus' lab origin? He told us it might dilute his narrative and efficacy of the response, but we don't know that for sure because the experts didn't allow it to be discussed. In other words, there is no evidence to suggest it would have reduced the efficacy of their response. Instead, he most likely shut down the conversation because Fauci directed funds toward gain-of- function research of novel coronaviruses at the Wuhan Institute of Virology, where the virus was made. How many people would have followed his advice had that been known early on? He had a conflict of interest the entire time and needed to cover his own ass, just like a good manager would. But Fauci is *the science*, as he once told us, because he is just a *man of facts* holding no true values. "I am somebody who only cares about science…" he actually said.

Facts are great, but the is-ought gap implies that they can never tell us what to do. The advice from a man of facts should be cautiously weighed against our values.

The risk/reward balance during COVID was never followed in the US. Our country gave up our values due to a lack of good leadership. Leaders must have good ideas, or at least know when something is a bad idea. This requires strong values.

Two St. Paul, Minnesota hospitals permanently closed down at the height of the pandemic, with 900 laid-off medical providers, despite hospital bed shortages and perceived risk of COVID consistently making the local news. Unfortunately, it didn't just happen there. Other doctors and nurses were laid off as "non-essential" medical services were halted. 1.5 million healthcare workers were laid off at the onset of the pandemic with the related closures, per the BLS. This was rationalized as these doctors and nurses may not have triage experience, and you cannot have someone inexperienced working on patients. I agree in normal times – I don't want an unqualified doctor or nurse caring for me. But this was a pandemic we had to shut down the entire country for – ALL HANDS ON DECK!

A clinical nurse is *good enough* in the emergency department when a virus is rampaging through our country, people are dying, and we have a doctor/nursing shortage. Our politicians approved immunity to the pharmaceutical companies making the vaccine, and they could have also approved malpractice immunity for doctors and nurses on a best-efforts basis for treating COVID patients. But they didn't. Instead, the government paid them not to work, forced more out of the profession with mandates, and now wonders why we have a nurse shortage.

After the vaccine mandates took effect and labor shortages worsened at hospitals and schools, New Mexico, New York, Minnesota, and other states activated the National Guard to fill the vacancies. This was not at the onset of the pandemic but almost two years later. We laid off doctors and nurses at the onset, couldn't cross-train them for lack of expertise during the height of the crisis, but the National Guard is appropriate when the shortages were arbitrarily created by government vaccine mandates later? The system worked exactly as it was designed, and for some reason, we re-elected most of the people who designed it this way.

We needed strong leadership during this time. True leaders want more than just the facts. They have values. They make reasonable decisions by balancing the facts and values, risks and rewards, and costs and benefits. They don't shut down the country and disband free speech because times are tough. They don't close down hospitals and lay off medical staff during a pandemic. They don't print $9 trillion to support their poor strategies.

We pumped almost 50% of our annual gross domestic product into the economy in a year-and-a-half, and all it produced was about a year-and-a-half of moderate economic growth and investment gains. 2022 was then plagued with inflation, asset price depreciation, and intensified geo-political problems.

This all stems from the world's *handling* of COVID and extends far beyond Trump, Biden, or Fauci. We lacked leadership. Bureaucrats, the media, and social media companies silenced dissent, pushed false narratives, and forced our leaders to repeatedly take unwarranted action.

Florida's Governor, Ron DeSantis, initially followed suit with closures. But as soon as he had enough information, he reopened his state. The Florida apocalypse anticipated by everyone else never occurred. He withstood threats and false attacks and did what was right. The state prospered and likely led the way for further reopening throughout the country when people realized the concerns were overblown. The same cannot be said of places like New York, California, and Minnesota, which used harsh COVID policies but minimal science to support their actions. These states' closures and mandates achieved nothing, and Florida proved that. Their leaders did exactly what you'd expect from incompetent managers, and they attacked Florida. They doubled down on their stance instead of looking at the real science. Their value wasn't doing what was best; it wasn't about science; it was about being right and shutting down dissent. DeSantis valued doing what was best (and perhaps showboating himself a bit). Just remember, you can't get COVID at a social justice protest, but you can get it at a lockdown protest. You also can't get it from a liquor store, but you can get it at a boutique. Gavin Newsom and Nancy Pelosi can't get it from a restaurant or salon, but you can. The Science!

Masks are mostly ineffective, but that doesn't stop the occasional driver, alone, from wearing one. There is no evidence to suggest you can catch COVID from yourself driving alone, nor that a mask would protect you from yourself. Beyond the obvious fact that if you have COVID you're already screwed, but common sense also tells us breathing in your own infected breath will not stop you from catching COVID and that you, imagine that, already have it! I joke because I doubt these people actually believe the science. Perhaps this driver is a leader and acts as an example for the rest of us. Yeah right…

More likely, they're just virtue-signaling. They value appearing to hold the correct values more than science, more than common sense, and more than the well-being of our

Ch. 18 Leadership

country. This is what much of "leadership" has been reduced to – *to seem to be*.

Conservatives mistake the left as being stupid – "How does wearing a mask while alone help you?" or "How can burning down a building be a 'Peaceful Protest'?" It's not stupid, and it's not a lack of facts. Instead, it's a matter of different values. The Left was unconcerned that your business was burnt to the ground or that the rioter Michael Reinoehl shot an unarmed Trump supporter point blank in the head. VICE News even gave the murderer an opportunity to tell his side of the story where he admitted it (it was also caught on camera). Left-wing activists later cried foul when he was killed by his arresting officers after shooting at them. His family is now suing for his death and will probably win because it's the Pacific Northwest. This guy was a full-blown piece of trash person. Activists knew he murdered an unarmed person in cold blood and shot at the arresting officers – but his victims supported the wrong president, so who cares? It's a values differential.

Leadership is doing what's right for your constituency, whether it's your staff of baristas, medical residents, the union you lead, a group of bankers, or the country. Doing what's right depends on your values, and as was earlier shown, never from facts alone.

Narratives are powerful tools that use facts to make specific actions appear indisputably correct when they are clearly wrong – like limiting speech during the pandemic. However, we know facts can never tell us what we ought to do. Values hold that responsibility. Managers, leaders, and politicians ignore the facts and often manipulate them whenever it is convenient. You're a person who follows the facts, always? You may as well put *leader* on your resume to describe yourself because you are a total jabroni who is easily manipulated.

Calling all *leaders* for the open position of Yes Man.

I received an invitation to meet with a senior executive at a former employer to discuss increasing veteran retention at the company. Veteran attrition was apparently horrendous and much worse than for civilian employees. I was thrilled they wanted my perspective. I made a few personal notes about how the culture compares to military culture and the potential problems that could create, but I also spent a great deal of time reviewing the Department of Veteran's Affairs research on the subject. This included surveys and data for why veterans stay or leave their employers and what they're looking for in a company. That's the highest quality of data available on the subject. I prepared my talking points and met with the "leader."

At the meeting, I was surprised the senior executive never asked a single question about my perspective, nor did she invite me to share my research. Instead, the executive spent a half hour talking about how much the company cares about veterans and how they want to select five or so token veterans within the company to do a rotation in their Chicago headquarters. The group would meet leaders from various groups and gain a broad understanding of the organization. Presumably, this would set them up for leadership roles later in their careers. Wow. She provides all the details, and the only question she ever asks me is, "Do you think that would improve veteran retention?" I respond, "Yes, for those five or so individuals. What about the other few thousand veteran employees who do not get that opportunity? Why would that help them stay?" She responded with something about how

Ch. 18 Leadership

representation matters and seemed to take offense to the question.

Perhaps representation matters, but I don't see the substance. All she was willing to do was improve opportunities for a few in order to manipulate thousands into believing the company cared about them.

What if representation *doesn't* matter? We often hear "representation matters" and accept it as a given. But this organization spoke about executives as if they were rock stars. It's an organization that sets up a meeting on the pretense of understanding the veteran perspective to improve retention, but the executive just spends their time talking about how much they care and what they're trying to accomplish. She cared so much that she never asked for the veteran's perspective. What if these "representatives" or "tokens" are pushed into the same culture once they're promoted to the top, never seek additional perspective, and are incentivized to work against veteran interests? If the chosen veterans are only there for show, what does this suggest about the organization's intentions with the broader group? When someone selects you arbitrarily, they own you. You owe your career to their goodwill, not yourself. What does this suggest about how they can manipulate you? The same goes for any non-meritocratic initiative, but it is especially dangerous here because they're using our veteran identities (as tokens) to manipulate others, which is why they thought promoting just a few would improve retention of thousands.

Nevertheless, I never heard anything about the matter ever again – no selected veterans, no leadership rotation for veterans, nothing. I have no idea if it was ever implemented. She was hoping to *seem to be* concerned about veterans. Corporate American leadership at its finest...

Ch. 18 Leadership

Chapter Exercise: Good Leadership

List the qualities of the best leader in your life.

1.

2.

3.

Chapter Exercise: Poor Leadership

List the qualities of a lousy leader in your life. Put yourself in their shoes and note why they may make their decisions.

1.

2.

3.

Chapter 19:
Dig Deeper

This book is about substance. Whatever you do, make it substantial. That doesn't mean grand. To make it substantial, you must dig in, find what matters, and create value – this is the key to replicable and sustainable private sector performance.

Our topics went far beyond talk of careers and business because sustainability requires a holistic perspective. If you don't know why you're putting in 80-hour weeks, it can't last. You cannot sustain strong performance if your partner doesn't support your goals or you're a bad fit together. And you will become easily distracted from your goals if you cannot see through the bullshit all around you trying to convince you to care about the cracks in the sidewalk or cats on the wall. The more capable you are of digging in and discovering what matters in all aspects of your life, the closer you will get to achieving your goals and answering, "What is the good life?"

Ch. 19 Dig Deeper

The great Greek philosophers battled with the question of *the good life*. They called it *Eudaimonia*. Many translate *Eudaimonia* to mean happiness, but that cannot be correct in the context of an overall life. Happiness is too limiting, only temporary, and not an appropriate goal for a good life.

Professor Patrick Grim of State University of New York at Stony Brook raises this same question in his lectures through the Great Courses. He seeks to effectively translate *Eudaimonia* by breaking down choices in life to build 1) "a life to envy" or 2) "a life to admire." He proposes that a balance between the two is required.

We all know what a life to envy is – the worldly adventurer who grabs life by the balls (my words, not the professor's). You may imagine the modern playboy on a yacht with beautiful women. The life to admire is different. Professor Grim uses the example of President Abraham Lincoln. Lincoln lived a relatively short and tough life, and he oversaw the bloodiest war in U.S. history just to be assassinated soon after its end. Hardly any of us want to experience that life – but it is a life of many accomplishments that we admire. Gandhi and Mother Teresa lived similar lives to admire, although most of us do not choose the pauper's life of service to others.

I am not a playboy, Lincoln, Gandhi, or Mother Teresa, and that's OK. I don't need to be grand. I have an amazing family, a lovely home, and a good job. I've traveled a bit, but primarily within the U.S. I don't know how well my life represents a life to envy or a life to admire.

I enjoy remodeling my home (did I mention that yet?), but you won't see me laying tile or putting up sheetrock with a smile on my face. I'm often swearing up a storm about some son-of-a-bitch piece of tile I can't lay level or about my back hurting.

Ch. 19 Dig Deeper

Few people envy re-tiling several hundred square feet of space – hell, I don't envy it. I tell myself, "I'm never doing that again" whenever I finish a project. My friends poke fun at me because I will start a new project just a few weeks after completing the last, and they certainly don't admire me for the effort.

That is not happiness. I do not define the enjoyment of the space afterward as happiness. I believe what I am experiencing is Eudaimonia, and it appears to be derived more from a sense of purpose than any outcome.

There are two primary factors for my Eudaimonia: Progress and Relationships. Progress is seeing improvement in whatever I am doing. Relationships involve getting to know people and experiencing life with them.

I skateboarded for 20 years. I loved skateboarding for the physical component and the identifiable progression. You either land a trick, or you don't. You try it; you don't make it; you try it over and over and over again, many times. It can take years to land a trick, but once you do, it's more or less muscle memory, and it's added to your portfolio of tricks you can pull out any time you want. You also develop a style over time, which makes it an art form. That is progress in a quantitative (the trick or portfolio of tricks) and qualitative sense (your style). It was the best.

It was also the worst. Progress takes effort. Effort is often no fun. I would try the same trick over and over again for hours, days, and even months if necessary. It stops being about fun after 20 minutes, and the smiles also start fading around that time. I continued to work on it for the challenge and the purpose it gave me. In his book *The Art of the Deal*, Donald Trump talks about what he perceives as the neuroses of great entrepreneurs, which helps them focus on mastering their business. I had that with skateboarding as progression (learning a trick) often became an obsession.

An inner ear problem destroyed my balance a few years back. No balance, no skating. Randomly losing my balance with no warning helped me discover that I do not entirely control my destiny – more practice will never return my balance no matter how hard I try.

I lost purpose for a bit, or at least part of my purpose. Skateboarding was a significant component of my life, and I was good at it. I spent 8 hours a day at the skatepark many days a week in my early teens and kept up with it for 20 years. There were consequences when a life-long love unexpectedly ended. I lost a similar purpose when I left the military.

I still had some purpose, and I tried to cope with the loss of skateboarding by helping my *forever wife* graduate medical school and gaining a deeper understanding of finance and banking. However, those are less tangible than jumping on a wooden board or putting on a military uniform every day. My forever wife was going to graduate with or without my help, and fully understanding a financial concept is challenging without practical experience – I am not learning just to take a test. Unfortunately, I put more focus on my work, neglected myself by giving in to whatever my employer asked of me, and became depressed and discouraged with banking, almost walking away from it all without another job lined up. I didn't even want to apply to another banking job, worrying they would all be the same.

In a world of *good enough*, it is very difficult to find purpose. We see others getting by with minimal effort and poor-quality output, and we think that's the goal. Or, we work ourselves to death thinking money is the purpose because we don't know what else to value. You work a dead-end job to make ends meet temporarily but find yourself in the same position three years later because it is good enough, and finding a more fitting role is hard work. You say things like, "it's not that bad", instead of "I love my job".

To fabricate a sense of purpose, your company tells employees they're *changing the world* or *revolutionizing banking* with their new 1.5% cash back credit card. Rather than paying their employees more, your company hires consultants to develop a pre-packaged set of company values and train culture-driving managers. The market attempts the same by selling you a *local* microbrewery with the same beer as every other brewery throughout the US that has been developed in the last 15 years (owned by investors who know nothing about beer but understand consumer trends very well). With this attitude, you may assume I am unhappy, but you'd be incredibly wrong. Seeing the world for how it is helps me manage my expectations and, counterintuitively, is how I've progressed rapidly and become happier.

I don't want to convince you to like what I like.

Values drive purpose and are different for everyone. I have friends who have gone to Europe by themselves to site-see. They loved it, and that's great. That's not something I would ever do. On my deathbed, I would never say, "Why didn't I go to Europe!?!" If you would, that's a sign you should do it.

A previous employer flew me to Portland, Oregon, for a business trip. One night, I explored the city alone and interacted with a few random patrons and the Rogue Brewing marketing team. I liked the engagement; they were interesting people, and that's essentially the only thing I remember about that night. The beer was good, but nothing I would travel for, and neither was the venue. I stayed with a co-worker's family for a few extra nights at their home/vineyard in Hood River. It's a beautiful area with a hefty river flowing between the forested mountains and a very peaceful, small-town feel. My most memorable experience was talking to this co-worker's dad about his vineyard, his hopes for it, and what makes a good grape while we shared a bottle of wine made from his stock. Those were connections and I loved that.

I find meaning in work. I like my job, learning about the world (which my job supplements), and progress. On my deathbed, I will gain satisfaction by looking around a remodeled room and saying, "I did this" – and awe at my efforts as I take my last breaths. I will also gain satisfaction by raising functional and healthy children and helping them live up to their potential.

I believe in working hard all of the time. If it's not my job, it's my house. If it's not my house, it's learning (my wife is tired of construction zones in our house, so spending my time studying is a better fit for her... for the time being). My daughter is now a priority, and a lot of work, but I still want to be productive elsewhere.

I'll decompress when I'm on vacation. Send me to a Mexican beach to sip on some margaritas. I'll take time to read, but with no urgency. If my wife wants to explore, I'll explore. Beyond that, I'm all good. That's one week per year, max, and I don't do things just for the sake of doing them.

The point is there are many ways to be satisfied. Do what you care about. Work if you like to work, or travel if you want to travel. Don't work hard if you don't want to, don't care about the benefits, or see no value in it. Finally, don't travel or whatever it is because you think it's what people should do. You do you.

Ch. 19 Dig Deeper

However, *you do you* does not mean you are good enough just the way you are. You're not. One of the biggest mistakes young people make is believing the popular narrative that people are fine the way they are and nobody needs to change – their uniqueness is valuable. This is garbage. This is why we educate our youth – they would be dumb if we didn't. They are not good enough the way they are. It is also why we practice skills, because poor quality is not acceptable. If we remember the earlier chapter about Progress and Stagnation, you will change just by staying you. That's not a good thing, and it isn't virtuous; it's narcissistic, and you're letting people feed on your narcissism for their benefit by telling you how good you are. You will attract the same types of narcissists as friends and partners. Have you ever heard of a narcissist reciprocating in a relationship? No, because two of them do not work well together.

You must put time in other areas to develop what you want more of. I could only have a meaningful conversation with the vineyard owner and the Rogue marketing team because I put the time in to learn to be inquisitive. Johnsons are not conversationalists by nature.

Similarly, bench press is a great workout to build your chest. However, if you aim to build a well-developed chest, you cannot only bench press. You cannot solely focus on your upper body. You need a routine that works out your entire body. Deadlifts and squats will release hormones and build strength that will help your chest despite using no chest in these workouts. You may not want to do these exercises – tough shit. That's what it takes if you want the chest. That is life.

My "successful" friend who built IT servers in his mom's basement quickly developed in one area. You can use his example of focus, planning and sacrifice to help you achieve your goals quickly. Many will never be fortunate enough to make a six-figure salary consistently. But there is a limit to how far he will go, and he peaked professionally several years ago. He's only 37.

A proverb states, "If you want to go fast, go alone. If you want to go far, go together." That friend is an independent worker, and his attempt to work with me on our IT consulting business and subsequent failure likely reinforced his inclination to go alone. But he has tried many ventures by himself that also failed. He always has good ideas but much less ability to sell. He also refuses to bring in other stakeholders who can help promote his work. Even if you have the cash to invest in your project entirely, it is probably better to bring in outside investors. You value full authority and reaping all the benefits, but no benefits can be gained if you can't sell your product. Give others an incentive to sell your product for you by giving them a stake. Equally true would be that if he focused on learning to sell like he did learning to build IT servers, he might be able to build a successful business. But he hasn't put in that effort, nor does he have a natural inclination for sales. He needs a business partner, and there's nothing wrong with that.

Our landscaping company was more successful than my dad's sole proprietorship. We accomplished more through the synergies of two hard-working people and more than either of us ever accomplished individually up to that point in time. Likewise, you can complete many home DIY projects alone, but an extra hand – even if it's just a gopher – can often help you finish more than twice as quickly.

My IT friend also valued quick and focused development and autonomy over traditional school. He dropped out of college when he realized he would make the same salary with or without a degree. This has also limited his growth. He is as

Ch. 19 Dig Deeper

equally skilled as many degreed professionals, but employers want to see that employees have invested in themselves.

I completed a program at NYU recently. Despite considering myself skilled, I did this at the recommendation of my manager. I wasn't offended he wanted me to continue my education. That's a sign he wants me to succeed and to gauge my interest in progressing. Education is objectively a good thing. I would be offended if he discouraged outside learning, as that would signal he wants me to stay put and under his control. An educated person has options – remember back to my discussion about my branch manager discouraging me from returning to school for finance and her losing her golden goose. Her manager probably discouraged her equally. Neither one of them is trusted with the same level of responsibility any longer. A leader who promotes your development wants you to succeed even without their involvement. Counterintuitively, that's the leader you should continue working for, despite having more skills that may qualify you for a higher-paying role.

When I decided to go back to school for finance, I considered many programs – JD, MBA, and a second Bachelor's with various business focuses. I considered top-tier local schools, private schools, and the C-school I attended for my Arts degree. (I call this a "C-School" because it was a public college with low entrance requirements and poor recognition. "C-school" is a play on "A-List" or "B-List" celebrities. If this school were an actor, it would sell non-stick frying pans on the Home Shopping Network at 2 a.m.)

I considered the time and monetary investment of each choice. The monetary investment included the direct costs and the foregone potential income with earlier graduation (opportunity costs). I decided on a Bachelor of Science in

Finance at the C-school primarily because 1) it provided the earliest graduation possible, 2) job prospects were good enough, 3) I would start in the same position with an MBA (even from a better school), 4) JD and MBA programs are too damn expensive, and 5) the job prospects for a newly graduated JD with no connections is far weaker than a random finance graduate from a C-school. I sat in on MBA informational classes and sessions at top public and private business schools in the area and found the curriculum wasn't meaningfully different from the undergraduate business courses I had already completed at my C-school.

Within the finance curriculum, I had to consider electives. Should I take Financial Reporting or International Finance? A bit of research showed a solid accounting understanding with a finance degree is a strong combination. Every finance major wants to work in stocks and bonds or investment banking, making six figures their first year, except very few actually achieve this. Those companies will also never hire a 30-year-old from a C-school with no connections. If they do, it's not likely to be me despite graduating Cum Laude. Did I apply for those positions? Absolutely, and I never heard from any of them. However, Commercial Banking loved me, and it was my preferred industry anyway.

My classmates had varying expectations: some wild and some dull. A young woman working as a teller at a bank hoped to graduate to become a personal banker. I cannot tell you your path is wrong, but that job requires very little, if any, financial knowledge, with the primary responsibility of reviewing basic income and credit score criteria and sales. I could teach you everything you need to know about personal banking within a day, and you'd be good enough and probably better than average. It certainly doesn't take a four-year Finance degree

This is like saying you want to study mechanical engineering to become a car salesman. An engineering education may help you in various areas, but that is the most challenging way to get to selling cars. As my Portfolio Management professor told me: work hard, but don't be a masochist. Understand the value of your program.

Another classmate was around 40 years old, had been working as a personal banker for several years, and wanted to become a stock broker/trader. We met for lunch about a year after I started in Commercial Banking. She had one year left in the finance program and needed some perspective on the job market. I explained how much I owe my position to taking the class Financial Reporting (now Intermediate Accounting I and II – they later split it into two classes because it was so difficult and extensive). Man, the professor was tough. On the first day of class, she introduced herself, discussed the massive drop rate by the end of the semester, and then went on to introduce our classmate Steven – whom she had the pleasure of teaching the class to the semester prior (he had failed and was retaking the course).

You know how college classes say you should expect to spend three hours outside of class each week for each credit (i.e., you will spend nine hours per week outside of class on a three-credit course), and it's total BS because you finish your homework in an hour? This was not that kind of class. I spent 13-15 hours on reading and homework per week outside of class. For our homework, we read approximately 100-page chapters, solved dozens of problems by performing the problem debits and credits, referenced the section of the book where we found the guidance for the treatment, and then referenced the FASB Codification website for the code that supported our answer. She was a solid professor, too; it is not like she wasn't doing her job. This class is meant to weed out the people who do not deserve to be accountants – there's a reason accountants are in demand.

Anyway, I suggested to my classmate that she take accounting because of the success it brought me (I only got a "B"), and it's the most practical of the potential electives. But she didn't want to do accounting and refused to consider that class. She wanted to focus on stocks and bonds. But she admits she's not very good at math either. She must be extra special because her goals clearly exceed her plans.

Five years later, this classmate is at a world-class institution working an entry-level customer service role.

This reminds me of the story of someone who wants to become rich so they can retire and drink margaritas on the beach all day, every day. I love that goal – margs on the beach. But getting rich is the most complicated way to drink margaritas on the beach. Why does this require that you be rich? The same goes for these women. Neither personal banking nor customer service requires a degree. Finance is one of the hardest degrees to obtain just to set yourself up for low expectations of life. The flip side is to have extraordinary expectations only to fail miserably. This classmate didn't understand why the program has the value it brings and the reality of our situation. We were all C-school students, not Harvard grads. I'm not saying we don't deserve the best, but this is why we must know what others want. The jobs starting in the six figures for undergrads are looking for the top graduates from the most prestigious schools. Set aside the school, is it believable they want the woman who refuses to do accounting and is only fair at math when they have an eager 22-year-old willing to work 80-hour weeks who double-majored in finance and accounting, knows three computer programming languages, and his dad is a VP at a large corporation? Those people exist, and there are entry-level jobs that require that.

Don't worry; you'll hit the six figures with a finance degree outside of the most prestigious career paths if you just stick to the program, do what's required, and stop thinking you're special (and therefore don't need the practical classes or skills). To this day, I wonder if she's stuck in her customer service job because she's not special or because she just refuses to accept where she is starting from and her own limitations, and therefore cannot progress appropriately (i.e., she drank the *you're fine the way you are* Kool-Aid, or *the world needs to change to fit me* mindset). I didn't hit the six figures until I was in my mid-thirties. Earlier in life, I thought it would come much sooner and easier, and I refused to acknowledge my limitations. My opportunities expanded as soon as I accepted my limitations, did what was expected of me, what was in demand, and just stuck to the program – the path is set, and I didn't lay it. People are already doing what you want to do. Find those individuals, analyze the situation appropriately (remember attribution bias), and follow their lead. You're not building a rocket to Mars – your shit's been done, that's OK, and progress begins when you acknowledge your constraints and the path that's been paved.

I wish I didn't have to take a year off from working at 30, start an internship, get a second degree, and work my way up from the ground level with 22-year-olds. Tough shit, that's what it took to change my life.

I have tried to help friends break into commercial banking as well. Banks need analysts, so I throw my friends a bone by teaching them a bit and setting up conversations with leaders. In their current roles, most of these friends are making less than I made in my first entry-level banking role, but they won't accept entry-level commercial banking. They want the same position I'm currently in, with several years of experience in the industry. I politely try to explain they're not qualified, but they don't understand because they don't understand what it takes. They never put 13 hours each week into a single class, worked 80-hour weeks, and all the other bullshit I've discussed. I'm trying to give them a good deal, but they want a better deal because they're extra special. They're so special they're in the same role I met them in almost a decade ago. If you're similarly stuck in the same position, not earning what you want, are you opening yourself up to incremental progression, or are you waiting for a great deal?

Despite warning you about the limitations of a C-school, do not believe your education is any worse than someone from Harvard if you went to a lower-end school. School is like a workout class – you get what you put into it. You can go to the most expensive Yoga studio in the world and not break a sweat if you do not try. I had some great classmates but thought many of my unprepared C-school classmates were a function of the low quality of the school and their admission standards. It wasn't. My Master's level classes at NYU were filled with the same types of jabronis, all admitted to a "New Ivies" school, and still could hardly grasp the concepts or follow the professor's lessons. Many of them NYU, Columbia, or other Ivy League or New Ivies undergraduates with comparable industry experience at the best companies.

In *Hillbilly Elegy*, JD Vance reflects on how difficult he expected Yale to be but was underwhelmed by the experience

Ch. 19 Dig Deeper

as he outworked and outsmarted the legacy Ivy League students. There is a perception of value from the brand, but many outsiders report the truth once they make it into these institutions, and it is always the same – it's a façade. Most of the trouble people like JD Vance or myself have keeping up is purely social, not intellectual or emotional – we cannot relate to the kid who was gifted everything. I've worked for the world's biggest banks, and I keep experiencing the same thing. I'm connected to the medical community through my wife. Want to know how many medical doctors are just idiots? Well, I am not sure the world is ready to hear that story...

The caveat here is any of the U.S. Military Academies – Naval, Air Force, West Point, ~~Coast Guard~~[1]. Military academies do not just educate based on facts. They instill integrity, physical and emotional excellence, skills, and values no other college can provide. You are not just educated but a professional warrior. That's tangible. We wouldn't need safe spaces everywhere if typical colleges taught emotional intelligence. Cancel culture would not exist. Politicians couldn't fight about student loan forgiveness if colleges taught tangible skills to every student because graduates would be able to repay the debts on their own. But many people just want the brand image a college degree provides. Brand – *to seem to be* (in many cases).

My wife and I were recently looking for childcare for my newborn. We came across a center that raved about the

---

[1] As an Air Force veteran, I feel it is my duty to poke fun at the Coast Guard when the opportunity arises. We take the brunt of too many jokes, and I'm using this opportunity to pass the baton.

background of their owners – Lululemon and Google experience. What does Lululemon or Google have to do with raising my child? They don't say. Will they impart some wisdom to get my child hired later in life? Probably not. The fact they didn't detail the positions held implies something not worth mentioning and unimportant. I can hardly imagine any beneficial experience unless it was running their corporate daycare or perhaps a teaching/training role. Despite these red flags, my wife still wanted to consider them, and we scheduled a virtual meet-and-greet. They never showeup to the appointment. Must be the Lululemon/Google standard. Or, they thought branding mattered more than the job at hand.

Be substantial. A name brand provides minimal actual value unless it represents something real. Toyota and Honda are known for great quality. McDonald's has a consistent burger. The U.S. Naval Academy produces the best college graduates.

FRED water is just expensive water.

Conclusion:

Find solid benchmarks and establish your standard. Do your own math. Not everything matters. Be substantial, but understand you are not special. You are going to have to work for it. Know the boss. Stop calling yourself a leader. Never do the wrong thing. Serve your country. Be clear. Just because nobody calls you on your bullshit doesn't mean you're fooling them. You're not fooling anyone. Be inquisitive. Don't accept the buck someone is passing. Take appropriate risks. Bounce back every time. Stop buying lottery tickets.

These are the lessons I learned the hard way after leaving the military. I wrote this so you wouldn't have to learn them the hard way or, worse yet, never learn them at all.

INDEX

12th Air Force / Air Forces Southern Command, 222-223
20%'r, 151, 163, 167, 190, 198
401k / Retirement Accounts, 48, 49, 53, 56, 60, 61
80%'r, 151, 153, 161, 163, 166, 167, 190, 196, 198
Acceptable Variance, 9, 10, 13
Accounting, 17, 73, 97, 111, 115, 177, 191, 192, 237, 260-263
Act Your Wage, 152
Agency Problem, 43, 153, 182, 186
AirBnB, 24, 25, 27, 80, 81, 91, 109
Alameda Research, 105
Amsterdam (film), 178-182
Antifragile, 29, 52, 74, 79, 88, 134, 240
Apple Inc., 17, 61, 182
Arbitrage, 61, 105
Assumptions, 3, 25, 70, 121, 143, 144, 145, 150, 197, 214, 222, 236, 255
Attribution Bias, 96, 204-217, 264
Automation, 234-235
Axiology, 32
B. J. Novak, 105
Baby in the Bathtub, 99
Banks / Banking, 17, 19, 40, 41, 42, 53, 62, 75, 80, 88-92, 97, 101, 111,
119, 122, 129, 130, 144, 145, 154, 163, 164, 170-177, 185, 191, 194, 200,
204, 206, 207, 208, 211, 212, 215, 236, 238, 239, 254, 255, 261, 263-265
Bankman-Fried, Sam, 105
Bedazzled (film), 39
Beneficient, 86, 87

Bible, 38, 40
Biden, Joe, 106, 181, 193, 201, 203, 244
Black Lives Matter, 44
Black Swan, 62
Bloomberg (media), 18, 93
Bumble, 116
Business Insider, 18, 19, 21, 30
Call of Duty, 65
Catfish, 108, 110
Certified Public Accountant (CPA), 36
Chance, 86, 92, 95, 99-101, 118, 139, 165-167, 213-215, 231, 232
Chappelle, Dave, 157, 158
Chief Executive Officer, 37, 99, 107, 179, 200, 238
Chief Financial Officer, 212, 237, 238
China, 44, 45, 103, 104, 164, 193, 197, 242
Civilization (game), 65
Cogent Social Sciences, 22
Cognitive Dissonance, 115
Competitive Advantage, 79, 132, 145, 209
Contractor's Triangle, 133
Corporate Class, 98, 197, 200
COVID, 27-29, 75, 78, 80-83, 88, 181, 229, 240-245
Cryptocurrency, 61, 105
Cuban Spies, 186
Daddy, 98-101, 149, 154, 194-200, 211-214
Davis-Monthan Air Force Base, 222, 240
Decision Fatigue, 72
Department of Veteran's Affairs, 145, 247
DeSantis, Ron, 45, 244, 245
DINKS, 78
Disability Benefits, 101, 145
Diversification, 52, 76-79
Don't Say Gay, 45
Dow Jones Industrial Average, 62
Effective Altruism, 105, 106, 107
Eliminations (accounting), 111
Eudaimonia, 251, 252
Excessive Risk, 61, 77, 78-84, 88-94, 99, 101, 131, 145, 172, 173, 209
Facebook, 86, 211, 212
Failing Forward, 135
Fake it 'til you make it, 98, 107
FDA, 78, 240
Finance, 11, 32, 41, 58, 67, 73, 74, 93, 97, 100, 121, 122, 134, 140, 141, 151, 153, 158, 164, 176, 191, 236, 237, 253, 258, 259, 260, 262
Financial Analysis, 17, 19, 21, 23, 40, 53, 58, 82, 154, 171, 187, 191, 233
Fit-ness, 114-124, 133-137, 143, 189

Florida State University, 22
FOMO, 5, 29, 91
Forever Wife, 34, 127, 136, 141, 192, 253
Fraser, Brendan 39
Fringe Class, 108
FTX (also see Alameda Research), 92, 105, 106
Fyre Festival, 92, 93
Gambling, 61, 79
Game Theory, 154
Gas-lighting, 166, 229, 232
Gajavelli, Jay, 82-84, 87, 88, 93, 20
Gen Z, 103, 104
Good Deal, 10, 26, 80, 81, 101, 105, 115-120, 132, 133, 152-157, 167, 207, 208, 264
Good Enough, 8-16, 21, 54, 56, 139, 185-191, 229, 243, 255, 257, 260, 261
Great Recession, 62, 75, 83, 89
Grim, Patrick, 39, 251
Gross Domestic Product (GDP), 111, 244
GuitarWorld, 105
GWG Holdings, 86-88, 93
Hedge Funds, 80, 85, 86, 238
Hedonic Treadmill, 48
Hillbilly Elegy (book), 264
Housing Bubble (see Great Recession), 83
How Universities Cover Up Scientific Fraud (see Dr. Justin Pickett), 23
Hurley, Elizabeth, 39
Influencer, 29, 84, 86, 103, 106, 215, 235
Innovation, 138, 150, 207
Investments, 16-19, 24-26, 29, 35, 41, 51-53, 61-64, 80-90, 116-118, 130, 164, 212, 213, 244, 259, 260
Investment Grade, 119
Investor Food Chain, 79, 81, 89
Is-Ought Gap, 40, 242
It's Always Sunny in Philadelphia, 68, 108, 114
Jabroni, 18, 24, 25, 53, 81, 142, 149, 175, 183, 195, 208, 246, 264
Juliobertos, 50
Landlording, 48, 53, 63, 64, 74
Last Marginal Investor, 89
Leader, 5, 17, 22, 23, 134, 138, 148-152, 171-178, 191, 200, 204, 209, 215, 222, 223, 228-249
Leadership, 149, 150, 171, 200, 209, 228-249
Leverage, 26, 74-77, 91, 128, 236
Liberal Arts, 4, 19, 20, 59, 109, 192, 193, 221, 259
Liquidity, 60, 87, 88, 90
Locus of Control, 186
Lopez, Tai, 109

Lottery, 6, 24, 26, 54, 65, 66, 79, 99, 103, 104, 114, 168, 194, 212, 215, 267
Low-Cost Provider, 132, 133
Luck, 3, 6, 66, 73, 77, 79, 81, 85, 95, 98, 100, 101, 106, 116, 142, 167, 199, 213, 214
Lyft, 86
Macro, 38, 57, 59, 60, 63, 65, 70, 74, 75, 81, 198, 199, 220
Madoff, Bernie, 92, 182, 183, 185
Magic Mike (film), 68, 69
Magic: The Gathering (game), 85
Malcolm Gladwell, 186
Managing Up, 166
Materiality, 17, 51, 60, 88, 149, 171, 187, 206, 233
Markopolos, Harry, 182, 185
McDonald's, 12, 215, 216, 266
McElhenny, Rob, 68
McFarland, Billy, 92
Medical Residents, 21, 52, 55, 56, 160, 175, 176, 229-235, 246
Men's Health (media), 59
Mergers and Acquisitions, 131, 236
Merit, 1, 148, 153, 165, 196, 198, 200, 248
Micro, 38, 59, 60, 63, 178, 199
Military, 1, 2, 4, 38, 55, 66, 71, 72, 163, 201, 203, 218-227, 233, 234, 247, 253, 265, 267
Minneapolis, 25-29, 61, 63, 109
MIT, 105
Morality, 99
Mulan (film), 45
Narratives, 5, 18, 22, 24, 25, 29, 31, 43, 44, 80, 85, 87, 89, 156, 157, 159, 181-186, 198, 205, 209, 210, 226, 240, 242, 244, 246, 256
Naturopathic Medicine, 20-22
Negotiation, 1, 10, 120, 128, 132, 155, 156, 159, 161
Nepotism, 100, 149, 167, 190-203, 214, 215, 228
Netflix, 158, 223
New York Times (media), 18, 107, 179-181
NPR, 42
Odd Lots (see Bloomberg), 93
OnlyFans, 61
Opportunity Cost, 27, 52, 58, 59, 61, 62, 82, 129, 130, 239, 259
Pareto's Principle, 151, 161, 190, 199
Passive Income, 24, 25, 53, 78, 82
Peace Ethics, 47
Pearl Jam (music), 34
Personal Finance, 121
Personality, 109, 138-147
Pickett, Dr. Justin, 23
Pivoting, 74, 133, 135
PLOS One, 21
Pokémon (game), 85

Ponzi Scheme, 92, 182, 183
POW/MIA Accountability Task Force, 223
Power, 10, 33, 39, 41, 101, 106, 125, 126, 135, 157, 160, 177, 181, 199, 204, 226, 246
Power Belly, 125, 126
Private Equity, 80, 81, 86, 87, 130
Public Markets, 61, 81
Public Service Loan Forgiveness, 42
Quantitative, 37, 59, 137, 162, 169, 196, 252
Quantitative Easing, 83, 122
Qualitative, 28, 37, 59, 148, 162, 191, 197, 252,
Rationality, 158, 159
Real Estate, 24, 27, 28, 30, 40, 45, 50, 52, 53, 59, 63, 64, 74-90, 106, 112
REIT, 78, 79
Replicability, 3, 5, 6, 29, 54, 74, 77, 79, 94, 168, 212, 215, 225, 250
Residency, 21, 54-56, 160, 175, 176, 229-235, 248
Resilience, 52, 134, 135, 140, 141, 147, 158
Re-skilling, 53
Retail Investors, 61, 86, 87
Return on Investment (ROI), 53, 212
Risk, 10-12, 29, 41, 42, 52, 60-62, 67, 74, 77-94, 99, 101, 119, 131, 132, 145, 156, 164, 171-173, 177, 185-187, 195 206-209, 220, 230, 232, 236-244, 267
Risk and Reward, 60, 61, 79
Risk-free, 62
Robert Half Salary Guide, 96
S&P 500, 52, 61
Search Engine Optimization, 139
Securities and Exchange Commission (SEC), 87, 182, 106, 183
Seem to Be, 103-113, 143, 149, 245, 248, 265
Seinfeld (TV), 167, 168
Self-employment, 11, 118, 121, 122, 130, 131
Selfie Wrld, 109
Silicon Valley Bank, 62, 88
Source Data, 16-31
SPAC, 87
Stanford, 105, 107
Stewart, Dr. Eric, 22, 23
Sub-Prime Lending, 119, 207, 208
Sunk Cost Fallacy, 134, 135
Taleb, Nassim Nicholas, 29, 52, 79, 93
Talking to Strangers (book), 186
Ten Commandments, 40
Tesla, 61, 234
The Federal Reserve, 18, 90, 93
The Good Life, 2, 4, 33, 68, 251
The Great Courses, 39, 251
The Greater Fool, 92

The Walt Disney Co., 44, 45
The Wrong Thing, 73, 175-178, 183, 185, 194, 267
Theranos, 92
Tides Equities, 84, 88
TikTok, 104
Tinder, 108, 116, 118
Tit-For-Tat, 154-156
Tradeoffs, 39, 46, 58-70, 133
Trading (see negotiation), 156
Trading (investments), 61, 105, 106, 130, 260
Trump, Donald, 43, 44, 181, 182, 244, 253
Trust, 19, 21, 118, 140, 142, 177, 178, 204, 218, 228, 258
Trust-Fund Babies, 50, 98, 211, 212
U.S. Bureau of Labor Statistics (BLS), 96, 158
U.S. Government, 16, 43, 61, 62, 81, 90, 92, 96, 111, 134, 179, 180, 181, 199, 203, 210, 239-243
U.S. Naval Academy, 8, 65, 192, 201, 221, 266
U.S. Navy, 8, 45, 65, 141, 192, 201, 221, 234, 266
U.S. Secret Service, 72, 73
U.S. Treasuries, 61, 62
Uber, 86
Uighur, 45, 104
Undergraduate, 19, 59, 259, 264
Underwriting, 89, 90, 170, 171, 178
Unforgiven (film), 158
Value, 1, 3, 7, 11, 12, 13, 16, 22, 27, 32-57, 60, 61, 65-67, 70, 79, 86-94, 98, 106, 107, 110-117, 127, 130, 133-136, 140-142, 148, 154-157, 167, 168, 170, 175-179, 187, 192, 194-196, 200, 206, 213, 225, 236-246, 250, 254-266
Value Creation, 93, 110, 111
Van Halen, Eddie, 104, 105
Vance, JD 264
Venezuela, 209
Vengeance (film), 105
Vice News, 246
Vision, 143, 234, 236
Vox News, 18, 21, 24
Wage Gap, 60
Wall Street, 37, 74, 82, 87, 130
Wall Street Journal, 82-84, 87
Weighted-Average, 239
Working-Class, 46, 54, 151-154, 192
YOLO, 61, 107
YouTube, 112, 215
Yuppies, 78
Zillow.com, 26
ZipRecruiter, 59

REFERENCES

60 Minutes. (2009). *60 Minutes Archive: The man who figured out Madoff's Ponzi scheme* [Video]. YouTube. https://www.youtube.com/watch?v=3wUJesUik5A

Agencies issue 2022 Shared National Credit Program review. (n.d.). Board of Governors of the Federal Reserve System. https://www.federalreserve.gov/newsevents/pressreleases/bcreg20230224a.htm

Ahmed, A. (2020, August 9). 77% TikTok users say that the app has helped them learn about social justice and politics, while 75% says it helped in discovering news. *Digital Information World*. https://www.digitalinformationworld.com/2020/08/77-percent-tiktok-users-say-that-the-app-has-helped-them-learn-about-social-justice-and-politics.html

Alba, L. (2022). Who is Tai Lopez? A scam artist exposed | Nomads MD. *Nomads MD | Work, Save and Travel*. https://www.nomadsmd.com/tai-lopez/

Aleem, Z. (2023, July 29). Opinion | Hunter Biden can't stop gifting the GOP with potential scandals. *MSNBC*. https://www.msnbc.com/opinion/msnbc-opinion/hunter-biden-art-sales-democrat-donor-identity-rcna96411

Anderson, M. (2020, May 10). Amid Pandemic, Hospitals Lay Off 1.4M Workers In April. *NPR*. https://www.npr.org/2020/05/10/853524764/amid-pandemic-hospitals-lay-off-1-4m-workers-in-april

Applesway Investment Group. (2022, February 4). *A message from Jay – founder & CEO of Applesway Investment Group* [Video]. YouTube. https://www.youtube.com/watch?v=_ee8oLngkeU

Aristotle. (n.d.). *The Nicomachean Ethic* (Translated with notes by Harris Rackham, 1996). Wordsworth Classics of World Literature.

Axelrod, R., & Hamilton, W. D. (1981). The Evolution of Cooperation. *Science*, *211*(4489), 1390–1396. https://doi.org/10.1126/science.7466396 Stanford University (1999). Axelrod's Tournament. https://cs.stanford.edu/people/eroberts/courses/soco/projects/1998-99/game-theory/axelrod.html

BBC News. (2019, October 18). Abominable: A DreamWorks movie, a map, and a huge regional row. *BBC News*. https://www.bbc.com/news/world-asia-50093028

Becker, K. (2021). Michigan Court: Sec. of State Broke Election Law with Absentee Ballot Order. *Trending Politics*. https://trendingpolitics.com/michigan-court-sec-of-state-broke-election-law-with-absentee-ballot-order-knab/

Bedard, P. (2021, March 9). Twenty-eight states changed voting rules to boost mail-in ballots. *Washington Examiner*. https://www.washingtonexaminer.com/washington-secrets/28-states-changed-voting-rules-to-boost-mail-in-ballots

Bond, S. (2021, February 8). Facebook Widens Ban On COVID-19 Vaccine Misinformation In Push To Boost Confidence. *NPR*. https://www.npr.org/2021/02/08/965390755/facebook-widens-ban-on-covid-19-vaccine-misinformation-in-push-to-boost-confiden

Brenner, L. (2021). Rated C for Censored: Walt Disney in China's pocket. *Harvard International Review*. https://hir.harvard.edu/rated-c-for-censored-walt-disney-in-chinas-pocket/

Brewster, J. (2020, December 16). Twitter To Remove Tweets Containing Vaccine Misinformation. *Forbes*. https://www.forbes.com/sites/jackbrewster/2020/12/16/twitter-to-remove-tweets-containing-vaccine-misinformation/?sh=3684758fe8cf

Buber, S. (2022). The most regretted and most loved college majors. *ZipRecruiter*. https://www.ziprecruiter.com/blog/regret-free-college-majors/

Chappelle, D. (2020). *Unforgiven* [Video].

Chuck, E., Walters, S. (2018). Tammie Jo Shults, who landed crippled Southwest plane, was one of first female fighter pilots in U.S. Navy. *NBC News*. https://www.nbcnews.com/news/us-news/tammie-jo-shults-who-landed-crippled-southwest-plane-was-one-n866951

Committee on Oversight. (2023). *New Evidence Resulting from the Oversight Committee's Investigation into the Biden Family's Influence Peddling and Business Schemes*. House.Gov. https://oversight.house.gov/wp-content/uploads/2023/03/Bank-Records-Memo-3.16.23.pdf

Corn, D. (2016). A veteran spy has given the FBI information alleging a Russian operation to cultivate Donald Trump. *Mother Jones*. https://www.motherjones.com/politics/2016/10/veteran-spy-gave-fbi-info-alleging-russian-operation-cultivate-donald-trump/

Covey, S. (2003). *The 7 Habits of Highly Effective People*. Simon & Schuster Audio.

Crime data. (2020). City of Minneapolis. https://opendata.minneapolismn.gov/datasets/cityoflakes::crime-data/about

Dalio, R. (2018) *Principles for Navigating Big Debt Crises.* Bridgewater.

Devine, M. (2023, May 9). CIA fast-tracked letter that falsely suggested Hunter Biden laptop was Russia op. *New York Post.* https://nypost.com/2023/05/09/cia-fast-tracked-letter-that-falsely-suggested-hunter-biden-laptop-was-russia-op/

Discredited Steele Dossier Doesn't Undercut Russia Inquiry. (2021). *The New York Times.* https://www.nytimes.com/2021/12/01/us/trump-russia-investigation-dossier.html

Doherty, N. (2023). Tai Lopez scam? Fact-Checking 37 claims (Updated). *eBiz Facts.* https://ebizfacts.com/tai-lopez-scam/

Dolvin, S. D., Jordan, B. D., Miller, T. W. (2015) *Fundamentals of Investments: Valuation and Management* (Seventh Edition). McGraw-Hill Education.

Dougherty, M. B. (2021, November 30). *Anthony Fauci: I am the science.* National Review. https://www.nationalreview.com/2021/11/anthony-fauci-i-am-the-science/

Durham, J. (2023). Report on Matters Related to Intelligence Activities and Investigations Arising Out of the 2016 Presidential Campaigns. *Department of Justice.* https://www.justice.gov/storage/durhamreport.pdf

Epstein, D. G. (2021) *Bankruptcy: In a Nutshell* (10th Edition). West Academic.

FDIC: Leveraged Lending: Evolution, Growth and Heightened Risk – Fall 2019 Vol. 16, Issue 1. (2019, updated 2023). https://www.fdic.gov/regulations/examinations/supervisory/insights/sifall19/sifall2019-article02.html

Featured Review: Physical interventions to interrupt or reduce the spread of respiratory viruses. (2020). *Cochrane.* https://www.cochrane.org/news/featured-review-physical-interventions-interrupt-or-reduce-spread-respiratory-viruses

Financial Stability Report – October 2023. (2023). Board of Governors of the Federal Reserve System. https://www.federalreserve.gov/publications/2023-october-financial-stability-report-purpose-and-framework.htm

Fischer, S. (2021). The Media's Epic Fail on the Steele Dossier. *Axios.* https://www.axios.com/2021/11/14/steele-dossier-discredited-media-corrections-buzzfeed-washington-post

Freeman, S. (2014). *The Art of Negotiating the Best Deal.* The Great Courses.

Fullenkamp, C. (2018). *Crashes and Crises: Lessons from a History of Financial Disasters.* The Great Courses.

Garfinkle, M. (2023, September 20). Gen Z's Main Career Aspiration Is to Be an Influencer. *Entrepreneur.* https://www.entrepreneur.com/business-news/what-is-gen-zs-no-1-career-choice-social-media-influencer/459387

Gladstone, A. (2022, April 4). GWG prepares for bankruptcy after missing payments to individual investors. WSJ. https://www.wsj.com/articles/gwg-prepares-for-bankruptcy-after-missing-payments-to-individual-investors-11649086394

Gladwell, M. (2013) *David and Goliath: Underdogs, Misfits, and The Art of Battling Giants*. Back Bay Books

Gladwell, M. (2019) *Talking to Strangers: What We Should Know About The People We Don't Know*. Little Brown and Company.

Grim, P. (2005). *Questions of Value*. The Great Courses.

Gold, J. A., Rossen L.M., Ahmad F.B., et al. (October 23, 2020) Race, Ethnicity, and Age Trends in Persons Who Died from COVID-19 — United States, May–August 2020. MMWR Morb Mortal Wkly Rep 2020;69:1517–1521. DOI: http://dx.doi.org/10.15585/mmwr.mm6942e1

Golden, M. (2022, October 25). State court rulings did not deem 2020 election 'illegal' | AP News. *AP News*. https://apnews.com/article/fact-check-2020-election-state-supreme- court-rulings-008127465796

Graham, B. (1973). *The Intelligent Investor, Rev. Ed: The Definitive Book on Value Investing* (Revised Edition). Harper Collins.

GWG WIND DOWN TRUST. (n.d.). https://gwgholdingstrust.com/

Hickey, W. (2013, July 17). The Math Behind McDonald's Monopoly Sweepstakes Shows The Only Properties That Really Matter. *Business Insider*. https://www.businessinsider.com/math-mcdonalds- monopoly-odds-probability-2013-7

Hourie, I. (2023, June 28). Facing cash crunch, Tides may call investors for more money. *The Real Deal*. https://therealdeal.com/la/2023/06/27/facing-cash-crunch-tides- equities-may-call-investors-for-more-money/

Hull, J. C. (2014). *Fundamentals of Futures and Options Markets* (Eleventh Edition). Pearson.

Hunt, K. (2014, October 9). What are the odds of actually winning McDonald's Monopoly? *Thrillist*. https://www.thrillist.com/eat/nation/mcdonald-s-monopoly-stats-and- probability-behind-winning-prizes

Ibrahim, N. (2022). Did Disney vow to help repeal the 'Don't say Gay' bill? *Snopes*. https://www.snopes.com/fact-check/disney-repeal-dont- say-gay-bill/

Jacobs, A. (2022). National Guard Takes On New Roles at Understaffed Nursing Homes. *The New York Times*. https://www.nytimes.com/2021/12/22/health/covid-national-guard-nursing-homes.html

Jay R. Gajavelli - CEO - AppleSway Investment Group | LinkedIn. (2016, December 1). https://www.linkedin.com/in/jaygajavelli/

Jean, T. (2023, July 27). FSU Professor Fired; Provost Says Research "Negligence" Caused Near "Catastrophic" Damage. *Yahoo News / Tallahassee Democrat*. https://www.yahoo.com/news/fsu-professor- fired-provost-says-090026000.html?guce_referrer=aHR0cHM6Ly93d3cuYmluZy5jb20v&guce_referrer_sig=AQAAAIPcBcvT7IUswNIVvXiD_jessJ02Ia-y6_l6bbMKccSrHO5ccTdMB0mEeuH1UEomu396G9St6MqkfjaRLsk3bHs50PLZsFhk8U8hQD2gAjyv2IhzkAHWbD00efR7xwPNyc01KEnBJRAew_1OxffmYbcd7Zc1Iy4n4nYum05c3j8U&guccounter=2

Johnson, B. (2023). LPM Apartments near Loring Park fetch $74 million Finance & Commerce. *Finance & Commerce*. https://finance-commerce.com/2023/06/lpm-apartments-near-loring-park-fetch-74-million/

Kahneman, D. (2011) *Thinking Fast and Slow*. Farrar, Straus, and Giroux.

Kauflin, J. (2022, November 19). How Did Sam Bankman-Fried's Alameda Research Lose So Much Money? *Forbes*. https://www.forbes.com/sites/jeffkauflin/2022/11/19/how-did-sam-bankman-frieds-alameda-research-lose-so-much-money/?sh=573cb83a44c9

Keith, T. (2021, July 14). Hunter Biden's Paintings Are Going On Sale, Drawing Critics Of Art And Ethics. *NPR*. https://www.npr.org/2021/07/14/1015895944/the-latest-ethical-pitfalls-involving-joe-bidens-son-hunter

Keller, G., Papasan, J. (2013). *The One Thing: The Surprising Truth Behind Extraordinary Results*. Rellek Publishing Partners, Ltd.

Kelley, A. (2020, June 17). Fauci: why the public wasn't told to wear masks when the coronavirus pandemic began. *The Hill*. https://thehill.com/changing-america/well-being/prevention-cures/502890-fauci-why-the-public-wasnt-told-to-wear-masks/

Kelly, B. (2023, July 13). Arizona broker-dealer that sold GWG bonds closing down. *InvestmentNews*. https://www.investmentnews.com/closing-broker-dealers-financials-were-horrible-239844

Kieso, D. E., Warfield, T. D., Weygandt, J. J. (2015) *Intermediate Accounting* (Fifteenth Edition). Wiley

Kirshner, A. (2023, September 20). The FTX downfall has reached new levels of Farce—All thanks to Sam Bankman-Fried's parents. *Slate Magazine*. https://slate.com/technology/2023/09/sam-bankman-fried-parents-joseph-barbara-ftx-collapse-lawsuit-trial.html

Linda P. Fried. (n.d.). World Economic Forum. https://www.weforum.org/people/linda-p-fried#:~:text=MD%2C%20MPH.%20Scientist%20in%20epidemiology%2C%20gerontology%20and%20geriatrics.,as%20keys%20to%20optimizing%20health%20for%20older%20adults.

Maine, S. (2018, September 11). 'It's Always Sunny's' Rob McElhenney reveals the brutal regime it took to get his 'perfect physique' for season 13. *NME*. https://www.nme.com/news/rob-mcelhenney-body-always-sunny-in-philadelphia-2377882

Malkiel, B. G. (1973). *A Random Walk Down Wall Street: The Time-Tested Strategy for Successful Investing*. W. W. Norton & Company.

Mancuso, V., & St Clair, J. (2021, November 2). The 'Actually quite simple' way Mac from Always Sunny got jacked. *Men's Health*. https://www.menshealth.com/entertainment/a21285961/its-always-sunny-in-philadelphia-rob-mcelhenney-jacked-fit/

Maragakis, L., & David Kelen, G. (2022, March 22). COVID vaccine side effects. *Johns Hopkins Medicine.* https://www.hopkinsmedicine.org/health/conditions-and-diseases/coronavirus/covid-vaccine-side-effects

Morning Edition. (2010, March 2). Madoff Whistleblower: SEC Failed To Do The Math. *NPR.* https://www.npr.org/2010/03/02/124208012/madoff-whistleblower-sec-failed-to-do-the-math

Napolitano, E., & Cheung, B. (2022, November 18). Sam Bankman-Fried and the FTX collapse, explained. *NBC News.* https://www.nbcnews.com/tech/crypto/sam-bankman-fried-crypto-ftx-collapse-explained-rcna57582

Neubauer, K. (2022, November 30). This 31-year old investor nearly quadrupled his multifamily housing empire from California to Texas in just 3 years. *Business Insider.* https://www.businessinsider.com/sean-kia-tides-quadrupled-apartment-empire-since-2019-2022-11

New data on COVID-19 transmission by vaccinated individuals. (2021, September 11). *Johns Hopkins Bloomberg School of Public Health.* https://publichealth.jhu.edu/2021/new-data-on-covid-19-transmission-by-vaccinated-individuals

Oluoch, T. (2023, June 15). Trend: TikTok activism. *Paramount Insights.* https://insights.paramount.com/post/trend-tiktok-activism/

Oversight Committee Republicans. (2023, October 2). *Comer Releases Third Bank Memo Detailing Payments to the Bidens from Russia, Kazakhstan, and Ukraine - United States House Committee on Oversight and Accountability. United States House Committee on Oversight and Accountability.* https://oversight.house.gov/release/comer-releases-third bank-memo- detailing-payments-to-the-bidens-from-russia-kazakhstan-and-ukraine%ef%bf%bc/

Palmer, J. (2020, September 12). Disney's "Mulan" disaster shows dangers to businesses of selling your soul to China. *Foreign Policy.* https://foreignpolicy.com/2020/09/10/china-disney-mulan-xinjiang-genocide-gap-business/

Parker, W., Putzier, K., & Shifflett, S. (2023, May 23). A housing bust comes for thousands of Small-Time investors. *WSJ.* https://www.wsj.com/articles/a-housing-bust-comes-for-thousands- of-small-time-investors-3934beb3

Pickett, J. (2020). How Universities Cover Up Scientific Fraud. *Areo.* https://areomagazine.com/2020/02/20/how-universities-cover-up scientific-fraud/

Player, N. (n.d.). The morality and practicality of tit for tat. *Pressbooks.* https://pressbooks.lib.vt.edu/pper/chapter/the-morality-and- practicality-of-tit-for-tat/

Pignatiello, G. A., Martin, R. J., & Hickman, R. L. (2018). Decision fatigue: A conceptual analysis. *Journal of Health Psychology,* 25(1), 123–135. https://doi.org/10.1177/1359105318763510

Pollak, J. (2022a). The most regretted college majors – and the least. *ZipRecruiter.* https://www.ziprecruiter.com/blog/the-most-regretted-college-majors/

Pollak, J. (2022b). The ZipRecruiter Skills Index. *ZipRecruiter*. https://www.ziprecruiter.com/blog/ziprecruiter-skills-index/

Popli, N. (2022, December 14). Here's what we know about Sam Bankman-Fried's political donations. *Time*. https://time.com/6241262/sam-bankman-fried-political-donations/

Pruni, A. (2020). Community fights potential loss of St. Joseph's Hospital. *Minnesota Spokesman-Recorder*. https://spokesman-recorder.com/2020/03/05/community-fights-potential-loss-of-st-josephs-hospital/

Putzier, K., & Parker, W. (2023, May 9). Bonds backed by apartments are under stress as housing market cools. *WSJ*. https://www.wsj.com/articles/bonds-backed-by-apartments-are-under-stress-as-housing-market-cools-9717d617

Qing, K. (2022, November 22). Bankman-Fried's FTX, senior staff, parents bought Bahamas property worth $300 mln. *Reuters*. https://www.reuters.com/technology/exclusive-bankman-frieds-ftx-parents-bought-bahamas-property-worth-121-mln-2022-11-22/

Reilly, M. (2023). LPM Apartments at Edge of Downtown Minneapolis Sells for $74 Million. *Minneapolis/St. Paul Business Journal*. https://www.bizjournals.com/twincities/news/2023/06/21/lpm-apartments-sold-minneapolis.html

Resnick, B. (2017, March 3). Study: half of the studies you read about in the news are wrong. *Vox*. https://www.vox.com/science-and-health/2017/3/3/14792174/half-scientific-studies-news-are-wrong

Reuters. (2023, March 10). Explainer: What caused Silicon Valley Bank's failure? *Reuters*. https://www.reuters.com/business/finance/what-caused-silicon-valley-banks-failure-2023-03-10/

Reyes, R. (2023, April 13). Florida professor leaves $190,000-a-year job following claim he faked data on racism studies. *New York Post*. https://nypost.com/2023/04/12/florida-state-university-professor-leaves-job-after-claim-he-faked-data-on-racism/

Roche, D. (2021, June 2). Fauci said masks "Not really effective in keeping out virus," email reveals. *Newsweek*. https://www.newsweek.com/fauci-said-masks-not-really-effective-keeping-out-virus-email-reveals-1596703

Ross, S. T., Westerfield, R. W., & Jordan, B. D. (2014). *Fundamentals of Corporate Finance* (Eleventh Edition). McGraw-Hill Education.

Schroeder, R. G., Goldstein, S. B., & Rungtusanatham, M. (2013). *Operations management in the supply Chain: Decisions and cases* (Sixth Edition). McGraw-Hill.

Sepic, M. (2020a, October 6). 2 St. Paul hospitals to close, psychiatric beds reduced in Fairview's shakeup. *MPR News*. https://www.mprnews.org/story/2020/10/06/two-st-paul-hospitals-to-close-psychiatric-beds-reduced-in-fairviews-shakeup

Sepic, M. (2020b, December 31). St. Joseph's Hospital staffers hope history of serving people in need will continue. *MPR News*. https://www.mprnews.org/story/2020/12/31/st-josephs-hospital-staffers-hope-serving-people-in-need-will-continue

Shiller, R. J. (2019). *Narrative Economics: How Stories Go Viral & Drive Major Economic Events*. Princeton University Press.

Shivaram, D. (2022, January 21). New Mexico is calling on the National Guard to fill in as substitute teachers. *NPR*. https://www.npr.org/2022/01/21/1074711399/new-mexico-national-guard-substitute-teachers-shortage

Singman, B. (2023, April 21). Biden campaign, Blinken orchestrated intel letter to discredit Hunter Biden laptop story, ex-CIA official says | House Judiciary Committee Republicans. *House Judiciary Committee Republicans*. https://judiciary.house.gov/media/in-the- news/biden-campaign-blinken-orchestrated-intel-letter-discredit- hunter-biden-laptop

Smith, R. (2023, April 26). Gen Z's dream job in the influencer industry. *NPR*. https://www.npr.org/2023/04/17/1170524085/gen-zs-dream-job-in-the-influencer-industry

S&P/Case-Shiller U.S. National Home Price Index. (2023, September 26). https://fred.stlouisfed.org/series/csushpinsa

Staff, R. (2020a, October 6). Fact check: Hunter Biden's military discharge was administrative, not dishonorable. *Reuters*. https://www.reuters.com/article/uk-fact-check-hunter-biden-not-dishonora-idUSKBN26M6QI

Staff, R. (2020b, October 8). Fact check: Outdated video of Fauci saying "there's no reason to be walking around with a mask." *Reuters*. https://www.reuters.com/article/uk-factcheck-fauci-outdated-video-masks-idUSKBN26T2TR

Stephens, B. (2023). The Mask Mandates Did Nothing: Will Any Lessons Be Learned. *The New York Times*. https://www.nytimes.com/2023/02/21/opinion/do-mask-mandates-work.html

Stevens, S. P. (2008). *Games People Play: Game Theory in Life, Business, and Beyond*. The Great Courses.

Stix, J. (2020). Eddie Van Halen discusses his early influences and groundbreaking technique in his first Guitar World interview from 1981. *Guitarworld*. https://www.guitarworld.com/features/eddie-van-halen-first-guitar-world-interview-1981

Table B-1b. Employees on nonfarm payrolls by industry sector and selected industry detail, not seasonally adjusted : U.S. Bureau of Labor Statistics. (2021, March 19). https://www.bls.gov/ces/data/employment-and-earnings/2020/table1b_202007.htm

Tager, J. (2020, September 16). Made in Hollywood, censored by Beijing - PEN America. *PEN America*. https://pen.org/report/made-in-hollywood-censored-by-beijing/

Takala, R. (2021). Twitter to Penalize For Saying Vaccinated Can Spread COVID. *Mediaite*. https://www.mediaite.com/news/twitter-to-penalize-users-who-claim-vaccinated-people-can-spread-covid-19/

Taleb, N. N. (2005). *Fooled by Randomness: The Hidden Role of Chance in Life and in the Markets.* Random House.

Taleb, N. N. (2010). *The Black Swan: The Impact of the Highly Improbable.* Random House.

Taleb, N. N. (2012). *Antifragile: Things That Gain from Disorder.* Random House.

Taleb, N. N. (2018). *Skin in the Game: Hidden Asymmetries in Daily Life.* Random House.

Tan, H. (2022, December 14). Meet Sam Bankman-Fried's family: His parents are Stanford Law professors, his aunt is a dean at Columbia, and his brother is the founder of a nonprofit. *Business Insider.* https://www.businessinsider.com/sbf-sam-bankman-fried-family-stanford-columbia-university-professors-ftx-2022-12#his-aunt-linda-fried-is-the-dean-of-the-public-health-school-at-columbia-university- 5

Testimony Reveals FBI Employees Who Warned Social Media Companies about Hack and Leak Operation Knew Hunter Biden Laptop Wasn't Russian Disinformation | House Judiciary Committee Republicans. (2023, July 20). House Judiciary Committee Republicans. https://judiciary.house.gov/media/press-releases/testimony-reveals- fbi-employees-who-warned-social-media-companies-about-hack

The "McMillions" Monopoly Scheme, Explained. (n.d.). *The New York Times.* https://www.nytimes.com/2020/02/03/arts/television/mcmillions-hbo- explained.html

Tillman, R. (2021, December 21). More states deploy National Guard to overburdened hospitals. *Spectrum News NY1.* https://ny1.com/nyc/all-boroughs/news/2021/12/21/national-guard- hospitals-covid-omicron-delta

Travis, G. (2023, March 3). How the Boeing 737 Max Disaster Looks to a Software Developer. *IEEE Spectrum.* https://spectrum.ieee.org/how-the-boeing-737-max-disaster-looks-to-a-software-developer

Trump, D., & Schwartz, T. (1987). *Trump: The Art of the Deal.* Ballantine Books.

Turner, C. (2019, September 5). Congress Promised Student Borrowers A Break. Education Dept. Rejected 99% Of Them. *NPR.* https://www.npr.org/2019/09/05/754656294/congress-promised- student-borrowers-a-break-then-ed-dept-rejected-99-of-them

Vance, J. D. (2016). *Hillbilly Elegy: A Memoir of a Family and Culture in Crisis.* HarperCollins Publishers.

Velasquez, R. (2022). Top Gun: Maverick made change that may prevent China release. *Game Rant.* https://gamerant.com/top-gun-maverick-taiwan-flag-restored-china-relcase/

Whitten, S. (2022, March 29). Disney vows to help repeal "Don't Say Gay" law, says Florida Gov. DeSantis shouldn't have signed it. *CNBC.* https://www.cnbc.com/2022/03/28/disney-vows-to-help- repeal-dont-say-gay-law.html

Why the US wants inflation: Why the US wants inflation, explained by fish. (2020). Vox. https://www.facebook.com/watch/?v=844408382816359

Wild, J. J. (2013). *Financial Accounting: Information for Decisions* (6th Edition). McGraw-Hill/Irwin.

World Health Organization: WHO. (2021). Side effects of COVID-19 vaccines. *World Health Organization*. https://www.who.int/news-room/feature-stories/detail/side-effects-of-covid-19-vaccines

Yang, M. (2023, March 17). 5 big moments from the week that rocked the banking system. *NPR*. https://www.npr.org/2023/03/17/1163911866/5-big-moments-from-the-week-that-rocked-the-banking-system

Zillow.com

Made in the USA
Las Vegas, NV
14 December 2023